MW01146132

WELCOME & THANK YOU!

Your investment in this book entitles you to a special gift that is the perfect companion to *Expressing the Divine.*

It is a group of videos that assist with meditation, expansion of your personal skills as well as a checklist to see what skills you may already possess and which ones you may be ready to improve.

This collection of media will allow you to study and improve your own metaphysical gifts in greater detail!

DOWNLOAD TODAY!

ThePracticalMystics.com/thanks

"You are cherished beyond measure. You are loved beyond measure. Now why do you measure yourself so harshly? When you love yourself as you are loved, the Divine becomes a beacon through you."

-Janine Bolon,
Crow Lodge, 2020

PRAISE FOR
EXPRESSING THE DIVINE

"*Expressing the Divine* gave me so much clarity on the mystical world. It helped me to understand my innate talents and to feel empowered with my gifts. Not only did I gain a better understanding of myself and of others, Janine provided concrete tools to enhance them and to integrate them into my every-day life. This book is basically a "how-to" for mystics, written by someone who has traveled the world and experienced it all in depth! I highly recommend this book for anyone searching to understand their skills and align with their purpose."

-Alison Repp
Mindset Expert & Mystic
www.LetGoAndFindFlow.com

"Janine has done it again! *Expressing the Divine* is written to give readers a roadmap to exploring, accepting and learning to use their gifts. She gives essential tools for anyone who is questioning their reality and figuring out how to navigate from where they are. I enjoyed the reminders of what growing your relationship with The Divine means for us as individuals and how that affects the collective. Brava,

Janine! You've hit the mark and provided much needed and very useful information for all of us."

"*Expressing the Divine* really cleared up some false beliefs and helped me resolve and dissolve resistance that I didn't even know that I had. What is meditation, what is this, what is that, what to expect, what to look for, how to feel, anything like that. Our awareness as humans is turning on to another level and Most have no Idea what to do or who to ask to get these answers. I love the chapter where Janine starts talking about The Clairs, -sentient, -audient, etc.. When I read that part it really helped me understand and differentiate some of the past things that have happened in my life and helped me understand other individuals around me. Thank you!"

ALSO BY JANINE BOLON

Seeking the Divine, Vol. 1

Finding the Divine, Vol. 2

Expressing the Divine, Vol. 3

Creating with the Divine Vol. 4 (Feb. 2022)

The Thriving Solopreneur

Money...It's Not Just for Rich People!

Ditching Debt

The Grocery Store Game

Cash, Cars & College: a YA Guide to Financial Freedom

10 Steps to Abundance: Mindful Money Mastery

DEDICATION

To all those who have come before me
To all those who have taught me
To all those who come after me
May you find the peace and joy I have
in your own unique way.

Published under the Copyright Laws of the Library of Congress of The United States of America, by:

The8Gates, LLC
1727 Main Street, #6386
Longmont, CO 80501-7311
720-684-6535

012621

CONTENTS

Acknowledgements 1

Preface 7

Chapter #1

Why I Wrote This Book 1

Chapter #2

The End of Sorrow 17

Chapter #3

Labels of Expression 33

Chapter #4

The Four Disciplines 43

Chapter #5

The Pleasures of Routines 57

Chapter #6

3 Minute Meditations 67

Chapter #7

Future Vision 81

Chapter #8

The First Three Levels of Experience 89

Chapter #9

The Choice You Make...99

Chapter #10

Cherished Beyond Measure 111

Chapter #11

Next Steps...123

About Janine Bolon..127

About The Practical Mystic Podcast......................129

Annotated Bibliography...131

Glossary of Terms Janine Uses..............................135

Personal Notes..139

ACKNOWLEDGEMENTS

A big thank you goes out to Mike Capuzzi and his team at Bite Sized Books who helped me get this guide into your hands so quickly. Without them it would have taken me longer to get this manuscript to press.

Also, thank you to the 24 beta readers who signed up to assist me with the flow of the book and the organization of the chapters. All of them were instrumental in how well this book reads rather than the jumping-around style that I write in. They helped smooth out the potholes and speed bumps for future readers.

A special shout out to the international members of the Crow Lodges and Divine MasterMinds that I have held over the past 10 years as I learned from other mystics, listened to intimate experiences of others in their walk with the Divine as I honed my own gifts. It has been an amazing journey hearing all of your stories. Thank you for the privilege to be in your lives engaging in topics you are unable to share with others.

Lastly, thank you to my children: Sean, Beth, James and Clare, because of their lives, their journeys and their perspectives, I was able to embrace the work I need to do while being a mom to them. Your understanding and laughter have kept me going when the rest of the world seemed bleak!

PREFACE

This guidebook is one of many possible answers to the questions you seek. I found what I was looking for on December 26, 2010. For most of my life I had a single overarching desire. I wanted an audience with God. I had some massive questions to ask Him/Her regarding the state of the world, why it operated the way it did and why I was here. These questions have all been answered for me and if my path can in any way give you clues to your answer, then it is appropriate for us to travel together for a time to see if any of my answers can support your own journey of seeking.

I am making some assumptions about you as I write this guidebook. Like any good guidebook it has to make assumptions otherwise how will you know if it is going to take you where you wish to go, right? As

I crafted out this book you'll find that it is written in roughly 3 basic sections, the first section describes the different definitions you are going to hear as people chat about metaphysics, spirituality, psychic gifts and the variety of ways that these gifts will manifest. The second section of the book will be discussing systems, tips and techniques that you can use to stabilize your own gifts and determine how best it is for you to proceed into new areas of this adventure we call life. The third section of this book is about you defining for yourself what your personal brand of truth is going to be. Yes, as a scientist you can see my training coming out here.

Many folks think it is important to find THE Truth for life (I should know, I used to be one of them.) I loved physics, mathematics, string theory and fractals as I saw scientists using the tools we had created to observe and describe the 3-dimensional universe around us. I loved this phase of my life and spent years learning and training my mind to be able to grasp the infinite concepts being presented to me as an analytical biochemist. Move forward 30 years and my mind & heart would be synchronized to a truth that was far beyond anything that my scientific peers could have described.

It is my goal to help you define for yourself the term mysticism. Because mysticism is experiential spirituality, unlike scholarly spirituality. Being able to study a book or scripture and integrate it is a skill that the scholars have, and I admire their ability to know the written word in such depth and to be able to translate what they read into a practice of spirituality.

The mystic, however, has a different canon. We may start off with a sacred text, but we know in our core that the Truth is hidden in our hearts not in the words on a page. Mystics choose to experience their God, Source or Creator through connection. So, no matter what religion you may belong to, no matter what truth you follow, mysticism allows all to gather in an understanding that truth is not an absolute. This makes many people quite upset, because they find comfort and security in the form of absolutes. The mystic understands better than most that absolutes don't exist in the realms of experience they have experienced. If anything, the sense of love and freedom experienced by the mystic causes compassion to be expressed by them in many ways the recipient of the compassion is unable to understand.

As you move through this book I'll be starting off with basic concepts that you may have already experienced. I do this so that we have common ground for the descriptions I will give further on in the book.

When you're done reading this book, I would

enjoy getting an email from you where you describe your own personal experiences. I would be honored if you would teach me your stories. Send me a note at Janine@the8gates.com. This way we, together as a community, can help others live the joy-filled adventure that they deserve.

-J.B.

January 2021

Master Mystic

noun

a person who has achieved by meditation or self-introspection unity with or integration into their Source. They know who they are and continue to become more expansive with each day they live. Master Mystics can manifest into their lives all that they need and desire.

CHAPTER 1

WHY I WROTE THIS BOOK

Lies, it had all been lies. As much as I would have loved to blame someone, anyone else for the lies that had been in my head, I couldn't. It had been all my own doing and there was no one to blame but me. You see, I received my enlightenment from my guru and Jesus-the-Christ on December 26, 2010. For anyone who has meditated for decades wishing nothing more than to be one with Source/God/All-that-Is, you know how amazing it is to finally know who you are.

This is an understanding without all the labels, self-delusion and self-identity you've created for yourself through a lifetime of living on planet Earth. You now know truly that you are one with Universal

Thought and there is nothing anyone can do to take that knowledge away from you.

However, what I was grappling with was the serious layers of lies that I had thought were my truth and as I watched my inner landscape turn to dust and my reality shatter into thousands of pieces of glass. I knew that I was in need of a different truth. One that was totally my own and if that made me "crazy" by other people's standards. That was not my problem anymore. I was done fitting in. I was done trying to explain myself, my gifts, my visions to anyone. I was going to create a beautiful world for myself and my children and I didn't care what I had to destroy, burn or wreck to make that beauty happen.

Hi, I'm Janine "Dancing Crow" Bolon, a scientist, scholar and psychic. I resisted my gifts for years as I sought truth from the only source I trusted. God. I am a recovering Catholic that left the church when I was 18 because I realized I needed a different path. I appreciate the Catholic Church for all they did for me. They grounded me in this physical world. I was a voracious reader of the saints and spent over 20 years studying the mystics of as many religions as I could. I made it a goal when I was 24 years old that I would seek enlightenment. I then found a guru and proceeded to sit in meditation, fast on a weekly basis and set my entire focus on my inner journey toward God rather than focus on making a career for myself.

I finished my degree in biochemistry and was employed by a University Laboratory. As I set off on a career in science I would spend my spare time reading stories of the saints, studying the journey of enlightened teachers throughout the world and reading religious texts to decipher this mystical mystery that is described as "Enlightenment." This was described as an experience where the human soul remembers their true identity from the Source that they came from. I wanted a one-to-one conversation with my Creator because I had a few questions for Him/Her on what was this Earth life thing all about? Whenever I spoke with anyone on the topic, everyone was as clueless as I was about why I was here? Why does the big "memory wipe" happen upon birth? What was I supposed to be doing? Just living? That was all too boring for me. I knew there had to be a bigger purpose to my life! Therefore, I sought answers directly. I wanted to chat with God. When I finally received those answers 10 years ago, they absolutely shattered my reality, I was left with pieces of my life and the pieces I picked up and brought into my new reality are perfectly harmonized, enjoyable and just plain fun! Life has become a beautiful adventure to me.

You are welcome to read the details of the search-and-recovery mission of connecting with the Creator in my other two books, *Seeking the Divine* and

Finding the Divine, but this volume is all about giving advice, guidance and suggestions to other souls who have awoken to their higher calling. If you have any sort of psychic ability (we all do, but some are more active than others), I encourage you to stop hiding those gifts. It is time to seriously create vibrancy with your life. This book will guide you to the reality that you are meant to create for yourself.

How to Use This Book

There are multiple ways you can use this book. It is meant to be a standalone guide to assist you along your path as you create a reality for yourself that is filled with fun, folks and festiveness.

If you consider yourself a mystic, psychic, medium, or some other label that suggests you get much of your information from this world as well as through your "sixth" sense, this book is written for you. You are already aware that there is a world beyond the physical 3D world society holds so dear. You are aware of your empathic qualities. You realize that you can either see, hear, taste, touch or smell (or you have all of these gifts at once) from other realms, while living in this physical world. The people around you do not always see, hear, taste or smell what you do. This sometimes can lead a mystic (my general term for those with psychic gifts) into thinking they are crazy. Let me be the first to tell you. No, you are not insane. As a matter of fact, you have opened the door to _leaving_ the insane world and are getting clarity on your true self and sanity.

As a shaman, scientist, scholar and psychic myself, I have spent the last 30 years studying, researching and journaling the stories, situations and successes of people just like you. As long as you think there is something "wrong" with you or that you might be "crazy," then I know you are doing okay. What feels "wrong" or "crazy" is actually the reality that is yours for the making. You know there is more for you in this life, you may just not know how to get where you are feeling you should go. The other maddening thing is that this feeling may come and go, and you have no idea what you're doing here on planet earth. You just know you came here to help people. The challenge is, it seems that most people just want to stay in their rut, not change, not expand or you find yourself in a situation where you just don't know how to dig yourself out.

Well, this guidebook is written in three parts to assist you in all these situations. The first part of the book is to help you identify some of the skills that you may have as well as open up your awareness to the many skills that are lying dormant in your heart. This list is by no means complete, but it is meant to be a foundation for you to experience all the different varieties that mystics have when it comes to their abilities and focus. I will share with you my definitions of the different spiritual skills and what you may be able to do once you get really good at listening to your own excellent advice. Meditation will help you with this.

The second part of the guidebook will show you some of the systems and processes that have been used by hundreds of psychics, mediums, and mystics to hone their skills and how they were able to increase their effectiveness, accuracy and confidence with the information they were receiving from their soul's awareness.

The third part of the guidebook is how to go about building a network for yourself so that you can increase your impact and really grow the number of people you can serve, assist and heal with your message while remaining financially solvent. As you grow in your spiritual skills, you'll find that having a supportive community is very nurturing to your soul.

A Bit of History on Yourself

You are an amazing being of light. You decided long ago that you wanted to have an opportunity to create a reality here on planet earth.

You picked your parents; you picked your surroundings, and you were a bundled ball of energy and light that was in extreme joy to be manifesting on the planet at this time. This is your time. You've been quivering with excitement for experience to happen. Now you are totally ready to make the next leg of this journey. This was the ultimate adventure for you, and you were all "in" to making this happen for yourself.

Now let's move to the different psychic skills and techniques you can learn to make your reality the joy-filled adventure it is meant to be.

Expressing Yourself

For most of us when you are given permission to "express yourself" there is a moment where you are stunned into inactivity.

There are a million thoughts, calculations and opportunities that are presented to you in that moment and you have no idea which one of the millions to do. Either that or your mind is totally blank, and you have no idea what to do. These moments of shock are due to the training we've had here on planet earth. We've been told so many times what is appropriate for us to do and what is inappropriate for us that we sometimes have no idea how to act for _our own enjoyment_.

Understand that this is done by people who care for us and they want to have our lives be easier, simpler and gentler than they experienced. However, your life will not look like theirs. Your life will be different. Way different. No matter how hard you try to play it safe, your life will be lived in a totally different way from anyone else on the planet. What I am recommending to you right now is this, relax. You don't have any disadvantages. You are not less than. You are exactly what you need to be right now. You are exactly in the right place, time and moment. By reading this guidebook you are taking the next step in your understanding and evolution into becoming an ever more deliberate creator of your own life.

When you make the choice that you are no longer going to live life by default, when you make the choice to live life according to your own inner guidance and you decide that the facts that you will follow are the ones that bring you joy, peace and excitement for life, then you will be building a life of your dreams. You will find after a bit of practice and some testing that you have learned how to make a life that is in your personal best interest. That, my dear, is an awesome life.

In the next several pages I'm going to be describing the labels I use when I meet, work with and integrate with other psychics and mystics in my network. I'm not saying these definitions are correct for you, but they are correct for me. After I woke up to my True Self in 2010, I realized that I wasn't the

8

only one that knew what I knew, and I started seeking others that understood the meaning of life as I did.

I found hundreds.

Over the course of the next decade, I would meet shamans, mediums, medicine women, healers, psychics and surgeons with incredible gifts. Many of them operated in secret locations and with nicknames because they were not safe if their culture, community or family, or if others learned of their extreme skills.

All the stories and experiences that I will share with you in this book are true. I saw these people; I have had them work with me or collaborate with me. Many requested that I not reveal their real names. I've come up with nicknames for them. Some of these shaman's gifts are so extreme that they don't teach anyone else how to do what they do, because the greed around them is so high that they don't want their abilities corrupted. They've already shared with me that they will die with the secret of their abilities. They hide their gifts yet have found ways to express them without any harm coming to them from those that would abuse them. You are quite lucky. You live in a world that allows you to express your gifts. You live in a world where you have resources, options and opportunities that were inconceivable to others just

10 years ago. Realize that your gifts are needed by others, so let's get you moving toward sharpening your skills. And as you sharpen your skills you'll be able to do it in such a way that you won't need to die with your secret to your psychic abilities. You'll be able to teach others, to share with others and to live with others without harm coming to you. That is the world we live in now.

Know that the life you wish to create for yourself is possible, but first let's show you what is available to you as an empath, psychic or mystic. Let's start at the beginning. When research was first being done with people that showed ESP or Extra Sensory Perception. Some basic definitions were made to help people communicate the gifts that psychics were manifesting. Let's talk about the foundational, basic 5 Claires. This is where we first notice our abilities.

Since we have the 5 Senses, if you find that you are receiving information similar to these 5 senses but in a different way then you have before, this means that you are now receiving information not from the 3D world, but through your intuition in addition to the information in the 3D world. It is helpful to discuss the Claires because they are very similar to our physical orientation, but each mystic knows that they are starting to get "more" from their basic five.

See how many of the basic 5 you have been using:

When you are calm do you have flashes of light at the corners of your eyes? Do you see something move like a shadow at the periphery of your vision? You think it is your cat or dog, but then you realize that your companion is actually at a different location in the room. Have you walked into the room and seen a flash of light and then assumed that it was just sunlight reflecting off the glass windows? Have you been doing a routine chore and had a full picture, like a scene from a movie flash through your mind's eye? The only difference was this time you knew all the people in the scene. And, lastly, have you started noticing that you seem to have issues with your vision, it blurs out, then comes back to clarity and then blurs out?

Put a check mark next to **Clairvoyance**. You are starting to see the astral plane while you are awake. Relax. Breathe and allow. This is a highly visual gift and one that creatives talk about all the time when they had a "flash" of insight on their latest sculpture, painting, logo or design. This "flash" is the skill of clairvoyance.

Moving on to other skills you may have. Do you hear things that others do not on an all-too-frequent basis? Have you gotten tired of asking if others "heard that" because you've been told "no" so many times? Have you had whole conversations you heard from another room and you knew no one was there because that was the guest room of your home? Do you frequently have ringing in your ears? This is **Clairaudience** and is frequently the skill used by mediums who speak with the dead. In your case, you are hearing things to get your skills tuned up. I recommend that you ask to speak to your Higher Self or your OverSoul and tune into the information that you receive at that point. We will discuss how to tune -in to this gift more later. As I write this my ears are currently ringing as I share with you this amazing skill. To get your ears to stop registering the ringing sound, I've been known to say out loud, "Okay, I hear you. You may turn the volume down." And the volume of ringing goes from a level of "ouch" to a level of "hummm."

Next on the list of skills is **Clairsentience**. I've described this as a "clear feeling." This skill starts off with you being able to sense the emotions and the environment around you. Many children who have parents with addiction issues are highly skilled in this area. They are used to walking into a room and "testing" the energy to see if it is safe for them to approach the addicted parent. They develop this skill quickly and it gets stronger the older they get. The skill becomes so good that when the mystic feels all alone or that they have been abandoned, they will feel a presence, feel a comforting hand on their shoulder, a hand brush their head, or they feel their hand being held. All of this with waves and waves of peace, safety and comfort flooding over them. Sometimes mystics are shocked by the sudden touch. But once you understand that this form of touch is always associated with comfort, safety and wishing you well, you will then be able to receive the flood of love, peace and understanding that is being gifted to you.

Clairalience (clear smelling) is directly tied to memory. Often, a mystic will be standing or sitting somewhere waiting for an event and they will smell something and a whole cascade of memory will shower into their awareness. Frequently, this is a positive memory of a dead relative or friend that they remember due to the scent they wore or the flowers they liked best, etc. These smells or odors will not have a physical source. The most common smells people have is of flowers, tobacco, food or perfume. Mainly from deceased friends or family, but as the mystic sharpens their skills, then the odors can alert you NOT to eat something or encourages you to drink something that you think might not be good, but then suddenly you smell sweetness, and you are aware that you are being guided by your Higher Self through your sense of smell.

The last Claire is one of the strangest I've ever experienced and that is truly saying something.

Clargustance or "clear tasting" has manifested in some bizarre ways for me. This Claire is related to tasting food, beverages, and air as cues using your sixth sense. Indulge me a moment here as I describe this gift from a personal experience.

I had been sitting at a restaurant surrounded by business associates when my coleslaw started to taste like pie. I knew that I was being shown by my Higher Self that this is how this ability works. I've had food taste like ash and I've had beverages taste like metal when my Higher Self was guiding me on what foods I should eat and what ones were not healthy for me.

I've also had the opposite situation when I was recovering from an illness and I had some food taste sweet so that I would eat it and others around me told me how bitter it was. Now the scientist in me knows how your brain could have deficiencies that would allow this sort of misrepresentation, biochemically speaking, as soon as I had that thought, I would "taste" the food normally and indeed the food was VERY bitter. I almost spat it out. This skill will assist you in your decisions on what foods are best for you no matter what others will tell you.

It is important that you listen to your intuition on this. Did you know that biologically speaking, when you lose the sense of smell, you also lose the sense of taste? Lucky for us, Clargustance and Clairalience are spiritually able to operate separately or in tandem depending upon what you need.

Now to the Bonus Claire. Some refer to it as a 6th Claire, **Claircognizance** or "clear knowing". This is not a Claire that is related to a specific physical sense for the human body which is why I don't discuss it here.

From this list of the Basic 5 Claires, how many have you remembered experiencing? I recommend you put a checkmark by each and then quickly write down those experiences that you remember for later on in the book. It will help you with the exercises.

☐ Clairvoyance

☐ Clairaudience

☐ Clairsentience

☐ Clairalience

☐ Clargustance

Use the blank area that follows to recall your own experiences.

CHAPTER 2

THE END OF SORROW

There have been many mystics throughout the ages that have awoken to their true selves. Each one had to come up with a lifestyle that would allow them to integrate with society.

Their awakened souls showed them the myth of this life and the power each of us have to create our own personal heaven on this Earth even while others around them saw it as a hell. There is an internal peace that emanates from those who remember their divinity and who are aware of the power they have over their own life decisions. Despite this knowing, there is the challenge of communicating this understanding with those we care about and our communities.

A Mystic is anyone who has learned that they are "more" than their physical body. A Mystic has personally experienced "more" of themselves and how they are incorporated into the physical world. They have experiences that solidify for themselves that are extraordinary, but they hide their talents due to fear, societal mores or insecurity.

Heinrich Zimmer is quoted as saying, "The best things cannot be told."

Unfortunately, he is quite right. What we have experienced as mystics is totally and completely beyond the realm of words. I remember in my own awakening process the use of language, or words in general, was stripped from me as I moved into the higher and higher frequencies as my soul (or Higher Self) guided me. The second thing to leave my awareness was the mental constructs we humans use to calculate time, space, and identity. All 3-dimensional constructs became instantly irrelevant, and then, emotions were stripped from my awareness. They, too, were a low frequency and I continued to move up the harmonics until all I was expressing and experiencing was the unconditional love of All-That-Is. I call this frequency—The Formless White Space of Creation.

Joseph Campbell says so well, "You can't talk about that which is beyond the reach of words."

Yet, here I am, finding myself talking to mystics about what I have seen, experienced and done. I make this effort to show those who feel alone, misunderstood and isolated, that there are thousands of us on the planet right now. I do this to help others remember the following.

No, you are not crazy.

No, you do not need an MRI.

No, you are extraordinary so please stop seeing yourself as normal.

Yes, you do hear things in the spiritual realm.

Yes, you can forecast what is going to happen next.

Yes, you have skills that are unique.

This is where mystics end up creating a sort of shorthand for the levels of frequencies that we experience. We come up with lingo in an attempt to describe what we know to be our personal truth. We know we experience similar things in the causal plane, but the way we each will express and share those experiences will be unique. The best we can do with one another is understand that we are beyond the realm of words and continue to walk in faith with each other that we know that we know that we know.

I describe the basic three levels of frequency of the mystical experience in my book, *Finding the*

Divine, but I'll quickly summarize here. Realize there are more levels, but I'll discuss the basic three as they have been taught over the past two centuries.

The Physical Plane—the basic level of human remembrance of who and what we are. Three dimensional spacetime where spiritual beings show up in bodies and experience creation in its many manifestations. The Earth Plane of experience is a carnival ride where we are humans that live on the 3rd rock from a medium sized star, spinning in a small galaxy made up of only 100 thousand stars. Tiny, by galactic standards.

The Astral Plane—the level where shamans, mediums, psychics and divinators operate with the six Claires. 95% of the mystics that I work with operate at this frequency. There is a lot of action and vibration here. It takes time and practice to weed out the noise (what we hear as silence or ringing in our ears) from the information we seek. It is the superhighway of the mystical world with an infinite number of stops, rest areas and non-physical beings offering assistance. Telepathy is used here, but language and feelings are transmitted at a faster rate than a conversation on the Physical Plane.

The Causal Plane—the last level before the soul loses all egoic identity and merges back into Source. At this level information is transmitted 100 times faster than the Astral Plane. There is barely enough "form" for each spiritual being to "see" with Clairvoyant eyes. At this level of experience there are zero barriers. All is love and because of that, you are 100% vulnerable. There isn't a thought, a reaction or a memory that isn't seen and available to all beings at this level. Privacy is non-existent. I've met very few mystics who have been here. The main characteristic of this level is the lack of judgement. It is total love here. Every thought, behavior and memory you have is cherished by the beings operating at this level. It is seen as "information" for others who wish to incarne in three dimensional spacetime. Nothing is judged. All is seen as perfect and beautiful. It can be a bit harsh returning to Earth life from this plane of experience.

As mystics we have plenty of challenges expressing and communicating with folks who are in the physical plane. It gets easier and easier for us to communicate with the Astral Plane, as that occurs, we then find ourselves in the position of articulating what we see, hear and experience on the Astral plane with those who are on the Physical Plane that haven't developed their mystical talents. You do your best to communicate, but the best you can do is be misunderstood when you first start expressing your abilities. It is maddening, isn't it?

Most people you are around when you first open up about being a "psychic" are operating in the first three chakras. (Chakras are portals of energy that the soul uses to express, incarne and resolve experiences.) People who operate in the first three chakras are either just trying to find ways to survive on this planet, they are looking for a mate to share their life with or they are busy creating a life of their own design and have no interest in what you wish to share with them. I have been fortunate enough to have met several other people who are awakened souls who have achieved a oneness within themselves and the known universe.

Mystics have several common traits and quickly cue into you if you share these traits with them.

1. We hear things, see things, feel things or taste things that others around us don't.

2. At some point we are labelled as "crazy," "a kook" or "weird" by someone we love. "Spooky" was my nickname for a while.

3. We are all quite active in the outside world and, yet, within each awakened one of us there is a point within us that is at complete composure and rest.

If our aspect of harmony or alignment is not there, as Joseph Campbell says, "we are in agony." For we know what unconditional love is, we have felt total acceptance and peace. We know of our connection to Source intimately.

This guidebook is here to help you with some of the language that has been built over the past 60 years. It is an attempt to describe the startling gifts souls are bringing to the planet in order to uplift humanity. You are a part of this process, otherwise you wouldn't be reading this book. Also, I wish to assist you with practical, solid systems and techniques that I use on a daily basis to keep myself out of agony and to keep my divinity where it belongs, in my heart chakra (the 4th one). I desire to have each heartbeat filled with compassion. My goal is to express that compassion with infinite patience and grace to all those around me. (I'm still working on the infinite patience part!)

Here are the most common questions that are posed to me when I first meet mystics and they reveal to me that they are "psychic." I basically created this book based on these elements alone because they are so frequently requested in my ceremonies and mastermind groups.

Here is your how-to-live-in-the-world guide after you have received enlightenment or have had a major spiritual transformation in your life. There are three things you will benefit from in reading this book:

1- Now that you know there isn't a god in the way you've been taught, how do you go about living your life? How do you keep from feeling like you're lost or have sand for a spiritual foundation?

2- Since enlightenment is different from what you may have expected, what do you do with yourself now that you know who you are, and all the layers of conditioning have been removed from your inner core?

3- How do you deal with the people in your life? Now that you can see them operating through layers of ego and fear?

I know there were times I was incredibly frustrated by the way I was brought into enlightenment and I wanted to read a guidebook that would help me get started with my new understanding of Life, the Universe and Everything. There are so many ways that a soul can open up to Source. I had a desire to come up with guidance that I could share as basic tips on how to handle life and move forward with your own new perspective and yet work within the flow of your current being.

It is my hope that this book takes you from where you are with your psychic gifts and talents to being able to fully integrate your abilities and live-in harmony with your current life. Some folks are so lost when they get their mystical wake-up call, that they really have no idea where to start or what to do next with themselves. I hope to sketch out some potential paths you can follow. For starters, let's cover the basic definitions that we will be using in this guide. It will help you to see where your talents are and the words that are used to define the characteristics you express.

Lingo for Physical Mediumship

The 6 Claires used to be lumped into the rather ungraceful label of, "The 6th sense" or "ESP" (extra sensory perception).

Over the past few decades so many new psychics have surfaced and better understanding of these talents have allowed for a better lexicon. I know I defined them for you before, but I have now reframed the definitions in terms of Physical Mediumship and how this relates to the other gifts that will be listed out later. The 6 Claires that I discuss in this book are:

1–Clairaudience (clear hearing)—the ability to hear sounds said to exist beyond the reach of ordinary experience or capacity. This is related to those that have the ability to hear the voices of the dead in their mediumship or angelic singing. You may hear words, music or sounds. The first time my clairaudience came online for me, I heard the tone of a bell. I would continue to hear bells or music and eventually could hear conversations miles away from where I was located.

2–Clairvoyance (clear seeing)—the ability to perceive people or events in the future or beyond normal sensory contact. This is where a mystic may see the celebration of someone or an accidental injury someone sustains several hundreds of miles from their location. It is the ability to have visions of past, present or future flash through your mind's eye (sometimes referred to as your third eye)

3–Clairsentience (clear feeling)—this skill set lends itself well to those who have the ability to feel another person's pain. This is where business owners or police officers get a "gut" feeling about a situation or a person that they just met. If you get the "chills" for no apparent reason you may be tuned into the emotional situation of another person. You have the ability to tune into the emotional energy of a person or environment.

4–Clairalience (clear smelling)—the ability to smell odors that don't have a physical source. Many mystics report knowing of a particular perfume or tobacco of a dead relative when they are alerting people to their presence. Smell is a strong trigger to memory, and this helps us to heal our past issues.

5–Clairgustance (clear tasting)—The ability to taste something that is not there. Mystics have reported that this ability comes from spirits attempting to communicate or remind a loved one of a specific memory or experience based on the food or beverage that was important to that memory. It is further information to the mystic that they are being loved and supported from the spirit world.

6–Claircognizance (clear knowing)—this ability is frequently a fact or truth just suddenly pops into your mind without any precursor. You just have a premonition without any rational explanation about how you "know" that particular fact. Many times, people "know" that an idea will or will not work based on this intuitive leap that they have. This is one of the more maddening skills to have because what may be "wrong" for the mystic will be "right" for all their loved ones.

The 6 Claires are the beginning of your understanding of the non-physical world and begin to introduce you to the other gifts that can come along after you start to meditate and build upon your latent talents.

The following list of talents or techniques are listed in alphabetical order. These talents are some of the areas your abilities can take you:

Apportation—The ability to undergo materialization, disappearance or teleportation of an object. I have personally experienced and manifested this ability. It usually happens spontaneously. Rose petals, coins, stones and pieces of nature such as leaves, or bark are the most common items that are apported in the beginning. Later on, as your gift develops, you will be able to apport bigger objects.

Astral projection or mental projection—The ability to voluntarily project the astral body to temporarily separate from the physical body. For shamans this is referred to as Shamanistic Journeying where information, healing or conformational knowledge is sought and brought back from the astral plane. There is a lot of misunderstanding and unnecessary fear surrounding this gift.

Automatic writing—The ability to draw or write without conscious intent. Many of the early mystics manifest this gift first so they could later harmonize with physical mediumship.

Divination—The ability to gain insight into a situation using cards, runes, pendulums, tea leaves, crystals or some other meditative tools or symbols. This is foundational to mystics building their own spiritual "code" to interpret what they are receiving from the astral plane. Eventually Master Mystics will leave these tools behind and don't need to build on their lexicon with Spirit.

Dowsing—The ability to locate water, sometimes using a tool called a dowsing rod.

Energy medicine—The ability to heal with one's own empathic etheric, astral, mental or spiritual energy.

Levitation or transvection—The ability to float or fly by mystical means.

Mediumship or channeling—The ability to communicate with spirits, talking with the dead, etc.

Precognition or premonition—The ability to perceive future events. Also called Clairsentience.

Psychic surgery—The ability to remove disease or disorder within or over the body tissue via an "energetic" incision that heals immediately afterwards.

Psychokinesis or telekinesis—The ability to manipulate objects with one's mind.

Psychometry or psychoscopy—The ability to obtain information about a person or an object by touch.

Pyrokinesis—The ability to control flames, fire, or heat using one's mind.

Remote viewing, telesthesia or remote sensing—The ability to see a distant or unseen person, place or thing, using extrasensory perception or Clairvoyance.

Retrocognition or postcognition—The ability to supernaturally perceive past events.

Telepathy—The ability to transmit or receive thoughts supernaturally.

Tools or Methods Use for Divination

There are several different forms of Divination that can be used by a mystic to retrieve the information they seek.

Below is a short list of the most commonly used methods that you can see at psychic fairs or spiritual gatherings. Please understand, just because a person uses tools, doesn't indicate their spiritual advancement. I have met many high frequency mystics at psychic fairs that had tarot cards, but could just as easily, "read" your aura by looking at you. The cards were their foundation. Make sense?

Astrology—The study of celestial objects as a way of gaining knowledge about human affairs and terrestrial events. Often the date of birth of the soul is used to determine the influences and challenges the soul has established for themselves in this life. The most adept astrologers I have seen are the ones that use 3-5 different astrological tools to determine the influences a person was living through. They can be quite accurate and give you a clear picture of how best to move forward.

Aura Reading—The aura is a field of subtle, luminous electromagnetic energy surrounding all living things in the three-dimensional universe. Some mystics can see it clearly, such as famous scientist, Michael Faraday, while others don't. There are psychics that can do aura readings and then interpret the results of the auric field. We now have cameras that record this energetic signature.

Cartomancy or playing card reading—This tool goes by many names that basically defines the origin of the card deck the psychic is using. Tarot Cards,

Oracle Cards or even a basic playing card deck may be used by a mystic to reveal knowledge.

Cleromancy—also known as runes, casting of stones, or rolling small objects and reading them by their position, orientation and mutual proximity. There are so many different variations of this form of divination that I have seen throughout the world. I, myself, used to have a bag where I kept my carved stone animals that I used for readings.

Distant Readings—are quite commonplace now, but it used to be that psychics had to be quite close to their clients to operate, but with the advent of technology, we have seen readings given via letters, telephone, text messaging and now online webcam readings.

Lithomancy and crystallomancy—used throughout the world that involve gems or stones that have been immersed in water or tossed onto a flat surface and are read by their mutual proximity. Recently, I've seen a resurgence in crystal gazing as it has become easier and easier to turn quartz into crystal balls. We've all seen the stereotype of a gypsy fortune telling in this fashion. Many mystics avoid this form of divination due to stereotyping, but it has its foundation in ancient meditation techniques.

Numerology—the study of numbers and number sequences and their influence on a client's life. Angel numbers, digital sequences and mathematical variants have frequently been employed to assist human life.

Palm reading—Palmistry is another popularized method of psychic readings. It is one of the techniques listed that doesn't require psychic ability. It generally uses cold reading abilities as a palmist studies the lines, shapes, wrinkles and curves of the palms and based on previous knowledge of the studied subject gives a client the reading. Palmistry is great for the mystic learning their personal lexicon.

Psychometry—certain psychics have the ability to obtain details about a person through the physical contact with their possessions. The belief is that objects which are in close proximity to a person for extended periods of time such as wedding rings, glasses, car keys, etc. hold some of the person's energy. This sort of divination saw a rise in the 60s & 70s and was highlighted in multiple events to locate missing persons.

Please understand that this list is just the basics of divination methods. I chose not to bring in the various tools that mystics can use for clarifying their readings such as pendulums, runes, rattles, drums, copper devices, oils, etc. This is a basic list to get us started in creating a language together of shared experiences. Also, if I use a word that you don't have a definition for, please look to the glossary to help you. Or email me: Janine@the8gates.com.

CHAPTER 3

LABELS OF EXPRESSION

B ecause of all the changes that our world is undergoing, there are more and more people like yourself who are waking up to their infinite potential. As they comprehend the increasingly expanding nature of who and what they are, they make the decision to express the divinity within themselves.

Here is a short list of some of the labels you may come across in your dealings with people from different cultures, tribes and countries that express their psychic abilities in a wide variety of modalities. Before I get into the list, I wanted to take a quick moment to let you know I've had the privilege of working with over 16 Native American Tribes, I've worked physically on 3 different continents and have had the honor of learning tools and techniques from people that normally found it best not to reveal their gifts to anyone.

This short list of labels and their definitions are becoming more and more muddled as I see our society evolve. Gifts and talents used to be strictly segregated. This is no longer the case. I'm seeing terms used in arrays of expression which can be confusing when you first are learning your own abilities. However, this list is a great beginning.

Psychic—anyone who has the ability to glean information from non-physical sources.

Medium—a person who talks to the dead or can have non-incarned beings communicate with them. Mediumship can be differentiated into multiple categories depending upon the person.

Mystic—Janine's general term for anyone who practices any form of the Clairs. I had to find a term for my community that didn't leave anyone out and didn't differentiate. This was the most general term I could find in the English Language that was broad enough to encompass all the gifted people I know. A Mystic is anyone who has a spiritual reality that is not apparent to the senses nor obvious to intelligence. Do you see how you fall nicely into this generality? Now, how you express it is up to you.

Medicine Woman—A tribal woman in charge of specific spiritual duties and healing modalities

Medicine Man—A tribal man in charge of specific spiritual duties and healing modalities

Seer—A psychic visionary that uses reflective modalities to forecast future events (smoke, water, glass, mirrors or fire)

Prophet—A recognized spiritual advisor to a community that gives guidance on present or future events.

Pipe carrier—This is tribal specific, but certain tribes have "pipe carriers" it is difficult to express their exact duties, but they are important to ceremonies where tobacco, herbs or healing plants are smoked to bring about specific results. The exact results are up to the pipe carrier, the pipe's energies and the tribal need. I have also met pipe carriers that were not related to any tribe because they had been "called" into service by spiritual promptings.

Wheel walker—A trained shaman in the healing and forecasting aspects of medicine wheels. This I have seen in many countries, not just the Americas.

Hoop Dancer—An individual whose ceremonial dancing can be traditional as well as healing to others watching.

Bell Dancer—An individual whose ceremonial dancing can be traditional, but some mystics change the environmental energies of a space by dancing in a region sectioned off for ceremonial purposes. This brand of dancing is not for entertainment, although it can be quite funny, bordering on hilarity, to watch.

Yogi/Yogini—A practitioner of Yoga. A bit of clarification is needed. There are several modalities of yoga. In North America's terms of yoga heavily focus on the physical forms of yoga. These are stated as exercise and flexibility practices. However, they come from a culture where these physical postures were used to prepare the body for long periods of seated meditation. These physical yoga postures were used by Yogi's and Yogini's to prepare for the other 4 forms of yoga that include meditation, breathing, energy and harmonization techniques.

Shaman—A healer that operates in the Astral Plane to bring about information and healing to their tribal members or clients. Shaman is an incredibly general term for tribal healers. Depending upon the nation, continent and country of origin, shamans will express healing in alignment with their traditions. Shaman is not a term relegated to Native Americans of North America alone as some would have you believe. Shamans are world-wide.

Sacred Clown/Court Jester/Heyoka—Heyoka is a Lakota word that describes a person that has been spiritually picked to be contrary to the tribal energies. These folks originally had to be struck by lightning or went through rigorous traditional ceremonies. Because of my heritage and life path, I was struck by lightning in the Bahama Islands while living on Eleuthera at a young age. I was found by Native Americans when I was 45 years of age, I first heard the term Heyoka in a vision when I was meditating. If you wish to learn more about the Sacred Clown/ Court Jester/Heyoka. I've written several articles on the topic. Here is the link to the most general one.

https://thepracticalmystics.com/2020/10/29/what-is-a-sacred-clown-anyway/

The gifts that you can express are endless, varied and have the potential to bring your quality of life into heaven or you can allow these gifts to lead you to hell. The choice is quite literally yours. When you remove the veil from your eyes, you are never able to go back to being your version of "normal" no matter how much alcohol you drink, cannabis you smoke or videos you watch. You will be able to escape into the 3D matrix for a time, but you will be called back into your purpose as you continue to expand your knowledge of all that you are. The point of me writing this book was to give you a bit of guidance so that you would not need to resort to escapism for long to bring yourself into harmony with your divine purpose.

If you are reading this book, more than likely you have a "practice" of meditation. I know you may not practice it every day and there may be whole weeks that go by and you don't do it. It is vitally important, now, as of this reading that you meditate each day.

You need time to quiet your mind and allow the mental chatter to calm down. I have an annotated Bibliography at the back of this book to guide you on some of my favorite books for meditation and the ones I use as reference. There are four books that are my "go to" time and time again as I assist my students. They are classics for me.

- *Ask and it is Given*, by Esther and Jerry Hicks
- *The Power of Now*, by Eckhart Tolle
- *The Four Agreements*, by Don Miguel Ruiz
- *Real Artists Don't Starve*, by Jeff Goins

These books are the foundation that I teach my students on how to get a discipline going for themselves. First, we focus on some form of meditation for them. I have an online course called 3 Minute Meditations that guide people into all different forms of meditation so that they can figure out for themselves what version will work best for them.

After you have figured out a form of meditation that you can use that allows you to calm the mental chatter in your brain (even if it is only for short periods of time) then I recommend these books.

Ask and It is Given is a great book that gives you the processes you need to take control of your emotions. Many of us were told growing up (and still are for that matter) that we are too sensitive, that we are too thinned-skin and we need to "toughen up." Most of the time this was told to us by family members or friends who saw how much we were hurt or injured by something said to us or the way we took the emotions that were behind the words. Ask and It is Given allows us to keep our sensitivity and abilities without forming walls, barriers and making ourselves become hard-hearted when all we wish to do is serve others.

The Power of Now is the single best book I have read when it comes to getting the mind to slow down and stop being so chatty when I'm trying to meditate. Eckhart Tolle's exercise of watching your thoughts like a cat watches a mouse hole immediately settles my mind's cacophony of thoughts so that I could rest in the peace and silence that ensues. This silence is where you harmonize with your Higher Self. This allows you to hear the guidance and support that is there for you and you alone. It is information totally customized for your life, your experience, your moment.

The Four Agreements is a book that is required reading for any member of the online networking groups I facilitate. It has been through this book that disputes have been moderated, disagreements resolved, and some members have chosen to leave the physical retreats that I have hosted rather than work within the four agreements. This is the point of this book to remind souls that we humans have been taught a lot of different things that are against what our souls know to be our personal truth. This book is what I use to keep harmony within a community and when disharmony occurs it is the reference book of "agreements" the elders have to assist our membership to work out their own internal shadows.

Real Artists Don't Starve is the book I use in my classes to assist fledging psychic creatives, artists and mystics to set up their businesses so that they can "make a living" doing their work full time. Over the past 20 years of travels this was the single greatest refrain I heard from every mystic I spoke to. Over and over, they shared the desire to do the psychic work "full time" so they could leave their "real" job. I wrote books to help them with money using the 60/40 principle and continue to do business coaching to this day in order to guide these amazing creatives into the realm of digital media, online stores, and marketing your talents to the demographics they wish to serve. When Jeff Goins book came out, I started using it as a reference in my classes to give more guidance to those who wished to operate full-time in their craft.

No matter what gifts you end up expressing first, realize that daily meditation is critical for honing your talents. Just like a knife gets dull with constant use, your gifts need to have the rest and renewal that daily meditation brings to you. There are many times when folks say they are too busy for mediation. Life has them running too hard and too fast. That is why I came up with my course, 3 Minute Meditations. You can find 3 minutes in your day to Stop. Sit. Listen. And by listen, I mean that you focus on the world beyond thought, beyond mind, beyond who you think you are. The world that is supporting your 3D experience, the world that is celebrating and encouraging your life experience every step of the way. The world that you may not remember because you've been so distracted getting used to the idea of what it means to be human and live life in safety and security.

CHAPTER 4

THE FOUR DISCIPLINES

In this chapter I'm going to ask you to give up on the idea of normalcy and realize one important fact. You are reading this text. That can mean only one thing. You are in harmony with the message contained within it. That means you are not normal.

Normal people think that they are living in bodies. They have no remembrance of the divinity within them. Occasionally they will have thoughts of, "Is this all there is?" "Where did I come from?" "Why am I here?" But these thoughts, these questions are too big a challenge for them to get into and they move on with their lives.

Take a moment to digest that, because this is an important differentiation between the folks who live life by default and you.

You, my dear reader, are living the life you have created.

You can accept that or not, but it is important for you to grasp the concept that if you are going to continue to grow, expand and increase your spiritual gifts that you move into the world of discipline. Now, discipline gets a bad rap. Someone needs to talk to the public relations department for the word, "discipline" because when I use this word, people shrink back from me and I can see them bring in dark thoughts.

Please understand that discipline is what allows us to create the life we want and if you don't have it, then start today to build upon it. Start today to create the life you want by working on the areas of your life that you wish to grow and become better. It may be as basic as, "I will become better at discipline." Most people know the most common use of the word discipline where they see it as, the training of rules, code of conduct and if you misbehave there is a punishment for you. Yes, this is true. That is the most common usage of the word. But remember when I said we are not normal? That's right it is time for you to rework some of the definitions you've created in your life.

One of the habits you have is the way you think of words that are being used by the people around you. Please start paying attention to the words as spiritual people speak to you and in the spiritual books you read. Realize that spiritual people who think like you, who aren't normal, exactly like you're not normal, don't use words in a normal way. We see them at their higher levels rather than the way folks use them in daily life. Day-to-day conversations have caused the use of some words to be changed. I've been amazed at some of the alterations to the English language in my short time on planet Earth. Let's get back to the word, Discipline. This word has two meanings, one is the common one, to punish someone for not following a code of conduct or a set of rules.

However, we're not normal so I'm using it in the other way. The way of the scholar, scientist and spiritualist. As Mystics, it is imperative that we have a form of discipline. This is what allows us to define for ourselves the way that we view reality, so called, and how we express our divinity to move within and around it. In order for us to truly make our life into the experience that is in our best interest, we will need to pull out all the stops and define our own discipline for our spiritual, mental, emotional and physical selves and stop taking the advice of those well-meaning people around us. These well-meaning people continually think that they know what is best for us. If you are reading this I'm making some assumptions about you. I assume that you are an adult. I assume that you have the presence of mind to know when you are feeling good and when you feel bad.

No one else can tell you if you feel good or if you feel bad. Right? I mean, really let's get down to basics here. No one can feel what you feel. Unless you are standing in the presence of a highly trained and sensitive empath who has gone through their training of discipline, no one can tell you "how" you feel. Even the best empaths I've been around have to feel a "shift" in the energy and they are getting their cues from other aspects rather than just your emotional state. The important thing to remember is, you are in control of your own thoughts and emotions. And this allows you to stay in awareness of what is in your highest and best good.

It is time to get you settled into a discipline of your own making so that you can improve and embellish the traits and talents you possess as far as the 5 Claires and the way you wish to choose to express your divinity. There are four areas of discipline that need development for the mystical talents you possess:

1. The physical discipline
2. The mental discipline
3. The emotional discipline
4. The spiritual discipline

I'm going to discuss these in the reverse order, let's start with spiritual discipline.

The Spiritual Discipline

The spiritual discipline is the part of your life that can get the most confusing because you're taking so many people's advice and it may or may not be right for you. One of the agreements that I have experienced between all mystics no matter their culture, heritage, clan, tradition or lifestyle is:

- We all agree that we are more than we think we are.
- We all agree that we are beings of light.
- We all agree that we are made up of unconditional love.

We run out of words, our conversations dwindle and when we mystics really try to discuss what we know from our spiritual experiences, we resort to using terms to define our unification as:

- The white space.
- The place without form.
- The place where only love is.
- The place of OM.

Things like that. For mystics who have remembered their divine heritage, there is no argument. So, what is it that I mean by the spiritual discipline of one's life?

Discipline—is the routine that you use every day to keep ourselves in remembrance that we are more than this life.

What do you do every day to remember who you truly are rather than what others tell you you are? No one knows you better than you. Right? No one knows your feelings, your thoughts, your dreams, your desires. You. You are the best person to know all of these things. Now, it is important that you come up with a routine that you do daily so that you can stay in harmony with your higher self or your remembrance that you are more than just this wonderfully, delightful human body.

What is the routine you use for this?

My discipline is composed of the following behaviors:

- Meditation (15-20min a sitting)
- Reading 20-30min a sitting
- I AM statements daily
- Journaling
- Sacred Movement (20-30min)

Let's move onto the second discipline that involves our Mind.

The Mental Discipline

It is time that you make the decision to get a hold of those vagrant thoughts that plague you. Just so you know, you are not the only one who struggles with these deep-seated dark shadows.

But it is time to release them back into the wild and stop them from domesticating you into thinking that you are "less." Because we both know you are "more." Much more. These are some of the vagrant questions that roam our mindscape without mental discipline.

Am I worthy enough?

Am I strong enough?

Am I abandoned?

Am I alone?

Am I the only one who feels this way?

When it comes to our thoughts there are certain thoughts that have been pre-wired into our brains. it is important that you take the time to dismantle the training you've been taught in "how to think."

As a college professor I spent years teaching students how to read books, how to express thoughts and how to manage the thoughts that would come into their minds as they read works that pushed against their personal, cultural & spiritual knowledge base. I would then tell them they were not their thoughts.

For you it is time to remember that *you are not your thoughts*. You are not your mind. You are more than the thoughts you think. It is time to become an observer of your thoughts. Here is a simple exercise to help you with this.

Sit in a relaxed state.

Rest your hands with the palms up on your thighs in a comfortable position.

Take a deep breath in through your nose and a double breath out through your mouth in a huh-huh sort of fashion.

Then move into your mind where your thoughts are.

As you move into your mind, imagine you are a cat.

You are a cat looking into your mind like it is a mouse hole.

You are looking at the mouse hole that is your mind and you are observing to see when the next thought is going to emerge.

As a cat you can sit with infinite patience

How long can you sit there as a cat looking at that mouse hole before a thought emerges?

This exercise teaches you to observe the thoughts that are not "you." Remember, my fellow mystic, you are NOT your thoughts.

This exercise is excellent during meditation.

The Emotional Discipline

Most of my life I was taught that as a woman I was not in control of my emotional state. Puberty was a nightmare as I tried to juggle my high school physics classes, mathematics and crying-jags over-nothing.

I remember the war between my head and heart. My compassion is strong for you, dear reader, because I know you fought and continue to fight with the issues and harmonization of your head and heart. Our emotional discipline is easy, in that, we know what we are feeling in each moment. The other aspect that is wonderful is that we can change our emotional states as quickly as we can change our thoughts when we discipline our routines and our processes. Let me explain.

No one can make you feel anything. There is nothing in the world that can make you feel. Our emotions are our choice. Where the challenge comes is in our triggers and how we have been trained to act when someone says or behaves in a certain way. As a mystic, you know that you can be sitting in a living room that is quiet reading a book and all of a sudden a wave of grief falls over you and you start to sob for no apparent reason. Or you are watching a video of nature and the next thing you know all you want in that moment is sex. Our emotions seem to pop out of nowhere and we feel like we have no control. These are emotions that happen on a dime, it seems. So, what is a person to do? The first emotion is not the problem it is the thoughts and emotional cascade **after** the first one that is within your control.

This guidebook is not meant to be a philosophical or psychological treatise on why emotions come from the subconscious or how to clear your past trauma. This guidebook is meant to give you tools, systems and processes to deal, in real time, any issue that may come across your inner landscape. When you deal with your own inner landscape, you can handle the outside reality manifesting before you.

Okay, so let's start with a scenario where you are doing great. You are buzzing along preparing something for yourself in the kitchen and as soon as you reach for a mug, you start to feel a wave of some emotion pass over you. As soon as you sense that wave, the common trait of empaths and mystics is to try to identify, "What is this feeling?" "Is it mine?" "Is it someone else's?" and then the next thing you know your thoughts and emotions are on a roller coaster.

The emotional discipline that is needed by empaths and sensitives is critical to their well-being.

What you feel is real. Yes. What you feel is important. Yes. But the discipline to pull yourself out of the basement of heavier emotions is just as important. Heavier emotions do not benefit you. The emotional discipline that I am going to share with you right now is so simplistic that some people ignore it or tell me that I'm a fraud because I didn't give them a "real" tool to help them. However, I assure you that this process works when you use it. The challenge is remembering to use it, right?

When you first feel the wave of heaviness pass over you as you reach for that mug in the cabinet, the very first thing to do is think this thought.

"What will make me feel better right now?"

Then you go do that thing immediately.

After you complete that action then ask,

"What will make me feel better now?

Do that action.

"What will make me feel better now?

Do that action.

You keep doing this until you find yourself harmonized to the place of contentment you were in before you had the wave of heaviness hit you.

This works. Try it and I know you will marvel at the simplicity as well as the strength this technique gives you.

The last discipline deals with physical aspects.

The Physical Discipline

The physical discipline is what many folks new to the path focus on, they work on taking care of their body, being strong, eating the right foods and dieting until they finally figure out what is the best course for their body, for their lifestyle and for their particular work.

They literally have to chuck out all the ways they are working on their food intake and output so that they can get some measure of control over their lives. This is the most basic form of discipline and there are days I still struggle with it. That is, until I learned how to really focus with the assistance of my clairvoyance and started having a conversation with my 148-pound future self and asked for advice from the person there.

Because there is so much confusion about "what is best for the human body to function on planet Earth" mystics are best served when they listen to their Higher Self, their OverSoul, however you wish to define the part of you that is still in unity with Source. Meditate, listen, and then make an action plan for how it is best for you to physically deal with your body, right now, in this moment.

Sometimes, you've had a very traumatic experience occur. Death of a loved one. An accident. An injury. That has put you in a place that you've never experienced before. As you move through this experience, the only control a mystic feels they have is over their physical surroundings and their body. This is where your personal physical discipline needs to come from your Higher Self. Contact the "you" that is in the future and has already moved past the issue you are currently experiencing. Talk to that future you of the action plan you need to move forward and then prepare yourself to put that action plan in place. Also, prepare yourself for lots of changes to the plan.

You're Higher Self wants you to have the easy road. Your Higher Self will walk you toward your future with ease and grace if you will relax and allow the guidance. The more you try to control you, the less effective the action plan will be that you were gifted. It is imperative that you meditate, relax, listen, breathe and listen and you'll eventually get exactly what you need to do for you.

An example I use all the time is coffee. I've been told my entire life that I drink too much coffee. That it isn't good for me. That I need to give it up. I did give up coffee for 6 months and in those 6 months I watched my thoughts spin out of control and I lost my grounding. It was then that I realized, coffee is a calmative for me. When I drink coffee, I think about the human hands that pick the beans, the men and women who walk those berries down the mountains, the roasters who roast the beans, the earth that yielded the beans. This form of grounding I do so quickly that I didn't even realize how I had managed to come up with a ritual, if you will, for physically grounding my gifts through the use of coffee.

I use this example to let you know you can have a physical discipline in anything. What do you do on a daily basis because it serves you well?

What do you do daily that helps you feel better?

Work better?

Walk better?

Eat better?

Focus on what you are doing well.

That is the first step in your personal, physical discipline.

CHAPTER #5

THE PLEASURES OF ROUTINES

The positive power of routine is indisputable. There is a lot of media shown of successful people that have gone out and made a wonderful life for themselves through the power of routine and discipline. I am one of those successful people.

However, others who looked at my life while I was building it, found my life to be boring or unremarkable. I have been labelled as a plodder by some of my coaches because of the systematic way I approached any challenge that presented itself to me. I wasn't the fastest person, nor was I the strongest, but because I am consistent in my approach and my behaviors I managed to be incredibly successful in all that I set out to accomplish.

Now, did I have failures in my goal setting along the way? Of course! You can't be successful without failing. Allow me to say that again, You can't be successful _without_ failing. The primary point to failure is this, what did you learn? Will you stand back up and try again? Are you going to give up on the vision you have for yourself and just lay there talking yourself out of your vision as being too big, too difficult, too tough? The answer, my friend, is try again. You fail, then try again. Keep standing up and be stubborn about your vision. Be too stubborn to give up. You are learning, you are getting better, you are appreciated for your efforts even though it doesn't feel like it at the time. The battle every successful person fights, is the internal battle in the darkness when no one is watching.

I am frequently asked how I am able to do all the things I do. Simple. I have routines. I have systems. I have processes. If I can't make something a routine, system or process then I don't do it for my life. I have learned that in order to make the life I want for myself; I am the one responsible for putting in the structure to receive all the things that the Law of Attraction has ready for me. If I am not in harmony with that, if I don't have the structure necessary to receive the blessings that are on their way to me, then I will not be in harmony with the opportunities once they arrive.

That was a lesson that came to me one morning in meditation after I read, *Ask and It is Given* by Esther and Jerry Hicks in 2015. The book has been around for years, but I had never read it until then. From this teaching I learned that I must be in harmony with the blessings that are already on their way to me. You must open up to the opportunities that are coming to you, but with the structure and processes that you need to handle the situations when they arrive. This is where preparation, opportunity and blessings all meet. It is synchronicitous and unplanned, but totally predictable when you work your way through it. It is a way to "get out ahead of it" as Ester Hicks states.

There are those who marvel at my discipline while others cringe and run in the opposite direction. I don't ask anyone to live their lives exactly as I do, but what I do share in my teachings, books and courses is the fact that there are many ways to go about working your life into the life you want if you will but take the time to decide what are the traits and talents that really matter to you. What gets you feeling tingly all over when you think about the thing you want to develop within yourself? What is the desire that you want to express through your life and your behavior?

That is what you go after. This is how you build your life around this topic, trait or talent. Now, many creatives like yourself have so many things you wish to do and you're afraid that if you don't act on your impulse immediately that you will forget about it and never get back to it. Some creatives look around their domicile at the ruin of projects and the unfinished false-starts of all the ideas that they had, and it sort of litters up their life with the detritus and wreckage from past actions of trying to work something out. We all struggle with clutter. Our lives in the nations where we have a high standard of living allows us the space and storage to collect things. This collection of things is not necessarily to our benefit.

It is time to ask yourself some questions: What is currently in your life that is not of benefit to you? What is cluttering up your space? Does your meditation room look like a museum of all these "things" that are supposed to be sacred, special or helpful to your spiritual growth? Would you like to know the most sacred thing in that meditation space? It is you. The most sacred thing in all the world is you.

The sooner you truly understand this from a spiritual experience the faster your peace, contentment and inner joy will bubble up for you. Christ, Buddha, Ganesha, Krishna, Mahavatar Babaji, Saints and Sages of all religions have come to me in my various meditations and have shared with me how each soul that is on planet right now is cherished, revered and loved for the creation they are building right now. And, most importantly, they mean you.

Please take a moment today and walk to a mirror in your living space. Look into that mirror. Look into your own eyes and say, "I am loved. I am loved. I love me." Watch and feel the emotions and thoughts as they play about your field and you will have a clue as to all the head trash that you have that tries to keep you from this simple, basic truth.

Another truth of equal importance is the power of your personal internal discipline. One way to access your abilities and power is to establish routines for yourself. When those routines get messed up, just follow them the best you can on days when you wake later-than-normal. The thing is this, by having routines in place your body, mind and spirit are getting out ahead of humans' tendency to live by default and you will establish a new wavelength for attracting the harmonious life you seek.

Over a decade ago I created *"My Perfect Week."* Now, I giggle every time I talk about *My Perfect Week*, because it is a joke to myself. Every Sunday Morning at 6am, I'm going through a list of questions asking myself how am I going to schedule my upcoming week so that my time spent throughout the week is in alignment with me and my children's highest and best good. For a total of two hours, my week is perfect. I have created a thing of beauty. However, as soon as Sunday afternoon hits, I'm already having to adjust my calendar and move things around as new data comes into my life about school changes, weather changes and the changes that life always brings to us.

Here is the list of questions I ask myself every single Sunday:

- Your Divinity—Meditation (How's it Going?)
- Body (Health)—What Exercise will you do this week? What food will you eat?
- Mind (Scholarship)—What are you reading? What are you studying this week?
- Heart (Creativity & Beauty)—How will you bring beauty to your environment this week?
- Family—Meet with each of the kids and schedule one-to-one time with them.
- What will make this week successful for you?
- How can I have more fun?
- How can I laugh more?
- How can I bring in more joy?
- Menu for the week.
- Build grocery list.

I've been working from home for over 25 years and I've established a weekly routine that works for me as I raised four children and ran multiple businesses. Roughly my general week would look like this:

1. Sunday—Planning the week, spiritual activities, reading, rest & renewal for the coming week's work.
2. Monday—Scouting activities and volunteering.
3. Tuesday—Meet with clients.
4. Wednesday—Meet with clients & Support Writing group.
5. Thursday —Meet with clients.
6. Friday—Paperwork, enter receipts, finish projects & email follow-up.
7. Saturday—Work on 2nd business 5am-9am, Spend the day with family.

There are routines to each of these days and I've given you the general idea of how I incorporate some of my systems for running my harmonious life. However, the two most powerful routines are my daily morning and evening routines. I do these so that I stay healthy, refreshed and energized.

Morning Routine

- Meditation
- Weigh in—stay in tune with the physical
- Coffee
- Write
- Breakfast with my eldest child
- Send Cards for an hour

- Exercise —Raja Yoga
- Shower
- 9am--->>> Start Work
- 5pm--->>> Leave Work

Evening Routine

- Brush teeth
- Pajamas
- Journal/read
- Meditation
- Sleep

I've heard some people say that my life has too much structure and that there isn't any room for spontaneity. How can I possibly have fun? I always look at them and state, "How do you know?" You can't just look at the routines in my life and make such statements. Until you live a life of routines you'll not understand the way The Law of Attraction will bring the spontaneity to you and fill in all the excitement, enjoyment and surprise any spontaneous creative will revel in. Seriously. What you are building with routines is a pleasure. The very structure of your routines are the tools with which to accept the FUN STUFF! The spontaneous joy! The unexpected abundance!

Decide today that you will build your own routines.

Decide when you will have your weekly meeting with yourself.

Decide what routines you wish to have for morning and evening.

Decide who is going to be your accountability partner for these changes (not your Spouse!) It needs to be someone outside of your "live in" person. If you wish to have someone like myself as an accountability partner, I offer group coaching twice a month with the Mystic MasterMind where we help each other stay accountable to the changes we are all making in our lives.

https://thepracticalmystics.com/programs

CHAPTER 6

3 MINUTE MEDITATIONS

One of the many challenges facing the mystic who is able to put himself/herself into altered states of awareness through meditation is the return journey to "reality." It is this experience of our souls having a life on planet Earth that causes us to second-guess ourselves and lose confidence in our abilities as well as our experiences. Let's discuss how to make tiny changes in your perspective to bring about huge results in your experiences and have the confidence needed to share what you know with others.

Once you've had that huge awakening experience, once you've been in the white space where you experience yourself in harmony with all creation and you've left the identification of yourself, your emotions and your thoughts, you arrive back in your life and you feel totally in love with everything around you. Yet, you understand that there are societal limitations for you expressing your unconditional love to people. They will misunderstand your intentions. They will vilify your intentions. They will curse your intentions. All of this because you are doing your best to demonstrate and express the Divinity that you've personally experienced. You are at a place in your life where you now know who you are, and you are doing your best to express the best version you can create of yourself.

Many of the lessons you've been taught as a child you are already unlearning. You've come to the understanding that not all the assumptions people have made about life on Earth are correct for you and you are now carving out time and space to create a harmonious life for yourself. I have met many mystics whose gifts were latent for decades and when they decided to live for themselves and create a beautiful life for themselves, their spiritual gifts seemed to explode around them. They had never learned about meditation or how to control the downloading information they were getting from their Higher Selves, so I frequently found I needed to give them some basic instruction on how "going within" and teach them a bit about how to meditate so they could focus and express themselves without coming off a floodgate of verbalizing information that caused others to flee from them. You know the situation when you talk straight for a solid hour and don't feel like you need to breathe! I know I'm not the only one who has had that sort of experience!

For those of you who are long-time meditators, please feel free to skim this section, but you may find one or two nuggets of information that will assist you in your own practices. My goal is to always find ways that are easier and simpler for people.

Why Should I Meditate?

Frequently this is the question I am asked by mystics whose spiritual gifts have just dropped into their awareness and they have no reference for what is happening to them. All of a sudden when the phone rings they know who it is before they look at it.

They can tell that the weather is changing without going outside, they know a friend will be popping by to chat before they call. Things like that. For them, meditation is something other people do, and they don't understand how it can benefit them. I ask them to meditate for 3 minutes a day for a week. If they don't understand meditation after that, call me.

Sure, enough they always call me, but it is always to gush about all the positive confirmations they are getting, the good things happening to them and how wonderful they feel after years of thinking something was horribly wrong with the way they were.

For you, a fellow mystic, and I'm going to make an assumption here, you've heard about meditation and even may have tried practicing it, briefly. The following pages are not going to be about "why" you should meditate, but instead give you some tips on how to meditate that will be easier on you and techniques that are simpler to use. For me, as a scientist, I've always practiced the techniques as they were taught to me for years, then after a decade, I was shown how to make the techniques simpler and more streamlined. I've presented these "updated" versions for you below.

Creating a Space to Meditate

Determine your location for meditation. It can be anywhere that allows you to focus and concentrate with some privacy.

Make sure that you have a chair without arms for your practice, this allows you to move your elbows and arms without hitting the sides of a chair. For years, I meditated in a closet with a tiny night light in the corner. I had a single chair that I used only for meditating. Anytime I was in my room and saw that chair, I was reminded of my commitment to meditate twice a day. The primary purpose of this particular chair and a location you only use for meditation is to help you focus on the purpose of meditation. To align yourself with your Divinity. It is to make sure you commit time each day to the "small still voice within" that gives you the comfort, peace and guidance you seek for your personalized life.

Carving out Time to Meditate

The next item on your "to do" list is to look over your upcoming 6 weeks. When in your day are you going to set up a time for your meditation? True, we are focusing on only sitting for 3 minutes each day to meditate, but when are you going to give yourself time to re-read these instructions and watch the videos I have supplied you in the reader's bonus that show you different ways to meditate?

You will need to make time to communicate with us (your online supportive friends) about your meditation and how you are doing as you move through the different phases of awareness. Let us know how you are doing, what is going on with your practices and did you have resistance to this contemplative activity? At least one of us has gone through it and will be able to give you suggestions on how to change your perspective, posture or circumstance to be successful with your end goal. Harmony.

Right now, look at your calendar and make the decision to establish an appointment with you!

You are worth the time.

You are worth the commitment.

You deserve the engagement this activity and community brings into your life so you can achieve the goals you've set for yourself.

Budget 5-10 minutes a day for the lessons and practices. When is that going to happen for you?

Pull up your calendar now and start making time for you!

Learning to Sit

I know it is funny to actually title this section as Learning to Sit, but as I have traveled the world and seen all the different ways humans move about their environments, it has become necessary that I remind you to sit in a way that brings the most relaxation to your body without allowing you to fall asleep while you meditate.

What I will be describing to you is how to carry your frame so that the muscles drape over the bones which will relax the body so that the strength of the spine carries most of the energy and allows you to focus on your spiritual side rather than the physical side of your life.

Remember that your goal for meditation is single fold. To calm the heart and mind so that you can hear your spiritual self-speaking to you in the pictures, words and emotions that are calming, relaxing and informative. Basically, meditation is simply active listening.

American society doesn't do this very well, so if you're an American you may need to give yourself some practice with this.

Sitting in Your Chair

It is important that you sit in your chair comfortably, but also while allowing your body to support itself. I was taught meditation very traditionally and then I had a guru who softened many of the techniques and I was able to be much more successful due to those changes.

I encourage you to find a chair without arms that allows you to sit up without leaning back and meditate. This was the way I was taught, but since then I've seen mystics who have used recliner chairs, coaches and other pieces of furniture to meditate in. They are all successful, but when I asked them about falling asleep during meditation, many of them had that issue.

The reason I encourage you to find a wooden chair without arms is if you try to fall asleep using the system I give you, you'll fall off your chair. I didn't have that experience until I had been meditating for 7 years, that was when I had started to achieve the state of nirvikalpa samadhi that is spoken of, all that you need know at this point, is it will take some practice to reach these states and until you do, I highly recommend a wooden chair without arms for your mediation. Once you reach these higher states of awareness you will crave those experiences over anything sleep offers you, I promise! When you reach that state of experience, feel free to use a soft, easy chair for meditation.

3 Minute Meditations

Start with only meditating 3 minutes a day. First thing in the morning and right before bed at night. Some people put their meditation chair right next to their bed, so they sit in it before their day begins and before they lay down for the night. Here is the process of settling your body for meditation:

- Sit on the edge of your chair so that your arms are free to move.
- Make sure your feet are flat on the floor.
- Keep your back away from the back of the chair.
- Lift your posture, take a deep inhale of breath and then exhale and relax your muscles.
- Drape your muscles over your bones, like you put a coat on a hanger.
- Take another deep breath in and let it out slowly.
- Begin your meditation.

Questions I've Been Asked

What do I do with my hands?

This is frequently the first question I get when teaching meditation to friends. It seems that we feel like we're up on a stage and that everyone is looking at us and we need something to do with our hands. We just don't know where to put them, how to hold them, so we end up clasping them in front of us, so we don't hide them in our pockets!

For meditation, the most relaxing place to put your hands is resting them on the tops of your thighs with the palms facing up. Depending upon the length of your arms relative to your torso, you may have to place your upturned hands at the junction of your thigh and torso or allow your hands to move forward a little to rest comfortably on the middle of your thighs. This will take a bit to figure out, but once you know it, your muscle memory will be locked in.

Remember the point of this. Your hand placement is used to help you with your posture. You don't want to fall forward in your meditation, and you don't want to fall sideways in your meditation. By having the backs of your hands supporting your straight posture, you literally have yourself locked into the most efficient sitting pose your body has ever been in.

You will feel your body give a sigh of relief that for the first time in a long time - it is at complete rest while sitting. <u>It is a marvelous feeling.</u>

What do I do with my feet?

Keep your feet flat on the floor. If the chair you have is too tall for the length of your legs, then place a blanket or pillow under your feet to keep your thighs as level as possible. That way as you increase the time of your meditations, the chair won't be cutting into the bottom of your thighs.

How do I meditate?

Since meditation is all about resting, relaxation and listening, some mystics really need some coaching on how to relax after a lifetime of doing everything but sitting still. For some people sitting in meditation is torture, so they don't do it. But for those of you wishing to progress your gifts, you'll quickly find ways to connect with your HigherSelf and be able to move into the deeper and deeper levels of consciousness without the need for movement over time.

After you are seated in your meditation chair. Take a deep breath in and let it go in whatever way is easiest for your body. Since the point of all this is to listen and not have thoughts roaming wild in your mind, remember to act like that cat staring at a mouse hole to see if any thoughts will try to come out.

If you find yourself thinking about anything, Take another deep breath and observe your thoughts again as the cat does looking at a mouse hole.

Set a timer and practice this for 3 minutes.

Inspiration from a Rug
and the Woman Who Carried It

An interesting thing happened in a hospital chapel...

I was visiting a family member after their surgery when I was 16 years old. I was quite uncomfortable with all the drama going on during this particular visit and had always found solace in Religious Spaces, so I located the Hospital's Chapel and ducked in. Out of habit, I pulled my rosary out of my pocket and held it in my hand to make it look like I was praying. In actuality, I was enjoying the silence and peace I always felt in places of meditation.

As I sat there various members of the staff came and went during lunch breaks and to pray before and after their shift work. At one point a Muslim woman came in with her prayer rug and initiated her spiritual discipline. I was fascinated and wanted to learn more but left the chapel and waited for her in the hallway. She was kind enough to spend some time speaking with me about her personal spiritual practices before her shift. That 20 minutes with her would change my life on the way I viewed prayer, discipline and the use of habit for my spiritual walk.

This particular woman said her Salah, or the Five Daily Prayers every day. She had a routine established by her faith, but her own desire for connection and the benefits that she received by aligning with her spirituality 5 times on a daily basis caused her to become quite joyful and animated as she described to me her faith, her prayer habits and her peace with Life. Some days required more prayers or different prayers, but she had a routine that kept her in alignment with her Allah, may his name be praised.

She told me of the Islamic prayers and what each one focused on, but I can't remember all the details. I've detailed for you what Wikipedia has to say about this format and it resonates well with my memory of our conversation so many years ago.

Salat, ritual Islamic prayer, prescribed five times daily:

- Fajr —the dawn prayer.
- Dhuhr—the noon prayer.
- Asr —the afternoon prayer.
- Maghrib—the sunset prayer.
- Isha'a—the night prayer.

I have seen this same sort of format of daily prayer used with Buddhists, Hindus and Jewish people. It is a routine of ritual that can be quite helpful in aligning you with your Source. My purpose for bringing this story and information to you is this.

Meditation/Prayer grows in strength and power with increased listening and practice. Your connection to Source is always there. It is our remembering that needs encouragement and attention. Here is a simple routine that will remind you to Connect with Source in any particular moment.

When you do remember to meditate or pray or your "chimes" ring on your phone's calendar calling you to meditate.

1. Rest in that moment:
2. Close your eyes.
3. Focus on your heart.
4. Do three of the breathing cycles using any breathing technique you prefer.
5. Tense your body.
6. Release the tension while doing a breathing technique.
7. Relax.
8. Rest.
9. Connect with Source.
10. Feel the Peace wash over you.

All of this can happen rather quickly. I have timed myself while practicing all these steps and found that I could complete them all in 25 seconds without rushing and I still receive huge benefit from the "break" in my day.

Why don't you really splurge and take a whole minute to do this 5 times a day?

Now, there's a crazy thought for you.

CHAPTER #7

FUTURE VISION

When I discuss future vision with a group of mystics many of them nod their heads and think I am discussing Clairvoyance. In most cases they are correct, but in this particular chapter, I'm asking you to dream a bit bigger for yourself. Future vision is for people who feel they have no control over their lives. They have totally forgotten their Divinity and they think that anything that happens to them is a fluke and had nothing to do with how they think, feel or react to their environment.

You, as a mystic, know better. You know you have the ability to change the energy of a room just by setting an intention before you ever walk into the room. You know you can create a calm, organized meeting by setting intentions, meditating prior to the meeting and not reacting personally to anything said in the meeting.

Vision Boards and Weekly Planning are the only way I have found to get things done for myself, my four kids and my multiple businesses. The months of January, April, July, and October sees me focusing on the changes I wish to make and how I want to implement them. I am looking at every quarter and making adjustments to my life and how I wish to move forward. The first two weeks of the year are all about the creation of vision boards for me. I like doing these things together and usually make it into a party and invite my friends and family to join me with vision board making. You'll find my living room littered with poster boards, scraps of paper, oversized pictures and calendars to track my physical, mental, emotional, professional and spiritual goals. How are you going to create your banner year? Well, here are some questions to get you started. Download this pdf file, "Dreaming Your Future Life" and answer the questions that call out to you most.

Dreaming your future life (free printable)

https://thepracticalmystics.com/expressing-the-divine-printables

1. Where do you wish to travel?
2. What type of job/work/activity would you like to do each day?

3. What does a perfect day look like? How do you spend your time?

4. What are the characteristics of your partner? Spouse?

5. What do you look like?

6. What do you wish to give back to the world?

7. What Is It That People Know You Do?

8. What amount of money do you want to have at retirement?

9. What people do you want to spend most of your time with?

10. What would you do if you knew you couldn't fail?

11. What are the things you'd like to have?

12. What types of people would you like to meet?

Your Future Begins With a 3 Step Process

Step One: Create the Dream

What is on your wishlist?

The Dreaming Exercise:

These questions I copied directly from Gary Barnes during his Breakthrough Business Bootcamp. (used with permission)

What do I want to do?
What do I want to have?
What do I want to give?
What do I want to be?
Where do I want to go?

Step Two: Create Your Personal Vivid Vision

Remember that vision is just the ability to see tomorrow today. So, what sort of life have you given yourself permission to have?

It is time to create your vision board, why, because a picture is worth a 1,000 words. Pictures allow you to emote what your future life will feel like in ways words are unable to express.

The 5 reasons every mystic should have a vision board:

1. They make you think about what you really want.
2. They help you get unstuck.
3. They give you a daily, visual reminder of your dreams.
4. They fire you up Emotionally.
5. They are just plain FUN!

Give yourself time to work with this step. Dream, Desire and Dare to be the person you truly crave to be with this exercise.

Step Three: Create Your Action Plan

Once you have created your wishlist, your vision board and have completed the pdf—*Dreaming Your Future Life.* You're onto the last and final step in the preparation process for creating your future life. That is, you break out a calendar of the year and pick 3 things off your vision board to work on.

If you are in debt, I highly recommend that you make the first item you work on, debt-free living. If you don't have any debt and all you owe money on is your house or your car, create a plan to pay off that debt quicker than you had planned.

Then pick two other pictures from your vision board and work on a plan to accomplish them as well. Maybe it is a trip to Hawaii or a college degree. Whatever is on the board, pick three items to work on.

Laying the Foundation
for the Rest of the Year

What I do next is the single best thing I have ever done to create the life I wanted and to change the life I was currently living. After I have done all the previous steps and have picked my three items to work on from my vision board, I print off the entire year with each month on single sheets of paper and I lay them out in a long line down a hallway and into my living room. Take the time to print out these monthly calendars and write down your future year. It slows your thinking down to allow you time to discover what you really want to happen this coming year. I usually give myself a half-a-day for this exercise.

You'll put down the known first. Write down on your calendar the items you know are "set in stone" such as school calendars, work holidays, travel and continuing education training and known vacation times. Now that you have the basics on your calendar. Look at your Vision Board again for inspiration. Where in your year can you start working toward the vision you have for yourself?

The key at this point is to make time to implement the things you know will bring you joy. As you look at the 3 items you wish to work on from your vision board, sit down with your string of months along the floor and decide what you are going to work on first and what you are going to work on second, etc.

Decide when you are going to start each project and what is the list of steps that you will need to perform. Worry "how" you are going to afford all this last. We are not interested in the "how" you are going to make this happen, we are only interested in "when." Here is a quick example:

1. If you want to learn to play the saxophone, put down the month that you will start searching to buy one to play.

2. Then schedule the next month to look for quality teachers.

3. Then the next month you start lessons.

4. By the end of the year, you'll be able to play 3-5 songs with this sort of step-by-step approach to growth.

5. You can make a goal that you will continue to expand your repertoire of songs at a slow and steady pace of learning one song every 2 months so that every year that you are playing the saxophone you are gaining 6 new songs. In the course of 5 years of playing you'll have 33-35 songs that you have memorized.

6. This is FUN!

Here is where you print off a year's worth of monthly calendars and work out a plan for your "Abundant Year!" Below are a list of links that will take you to free printable calendars:

Calendar-12.com or **Print-a-Calendar.com** or **Calendarpedia.com.**

The point of using future vision is to help you see that living life by default is not an enjoyable nor an easy task. What makes life more enjoyable is learning how much control you have in the creation of your own life, but it only starts when you know what you want and as you focus on what you wish to do, have, accomplish and be, you'll see the Universe bend to your will. Trust me these systems work.

Now that you have integrated how you wish to live your future life, let's go back to reminding you why you are here on Planet Earth to begin with.

CHAPTER 8

THE FIRST THREE LEVELS OF EXPERIENCE

When you are a soul who has totally awakened to All-That-Is, the ride back into your body is bumpy and chocked full of lessons on how your soul entered the body before birth, it is no wonder that some of these souls come off as a bit crazy once they are back fully integrated into their bodies again.

If you don't know what I'm talking about you are welcome to refer to the description of the full experience of my awakening process in *Finding the Divine* where I take several chapters sharing with you how I learned of the different levels of Divinity. I add my story to the many other stories of souls who are shown how we move from the soul state to the physical state and become humans.

For the purposes of this book, I will go through the different levels of awareness as I experienced them so that you have a bit of a map as you move through the different understandings of your soul's journey back to source while you still inhabit your body. Many mystics go through these levels of soul awareness and have no vocabulary for what has happened to them. Over the past decade I've spent hours foraging words to match the experiences. As many of you already know, the first thing to leave your consciousness as you rise to the higher planes of existence is, words! Words totally leave your awareness. It makes it incredibly difficult to express what you've seen and where you've "been." Right?

When I was first on the spiritual path in earnest, I read a book by Paramahansa Yogananda, "The Autobiography of a Yogi" in that book, he stated that there were three levels of metaphysical experience. Please remember Yogananda was writing during the 1940s and 50s so he had to keep things very simple because the 60s hadn't happened yet and he was one of the first teachers from India to arrive on United States soil to teach this "thing" called meditation. He was encouraging people to connect with their Divinity. This was a new and radical concept to most of the people he was speaking with.

From Yognanda's book, I learned of our physical body, our astral body and our causal bodies. This is how he described your experience as you move through the different stages of your personal awareness of All-That-You-Are.

The physical body is what most people identify with and they are perfectly happy to go through life, living, experiencing and dreaming all about their physical lives and only rarely do they ever ask themselves:

Why am I here?

What is the meaning of my life?

What am I?

This form of introspection was left to philosophers and wasn't something that anyone should bother with if you were a "working joe." But in this case we are talking about you, aren't we? As a person who reads metaphysical books, you know there is more. There is a veil of ignorance over your understanding and you are seeking to pierce through that veil of ignorance, and you wish to remember more about who you are.

The astral body was next on Yogananda's list of metaphysical elements. This body runs around the Astral plane. When a mystic is in this region of experience, they are still in their body, but they have calmed it enough that they are able to experience the reality behind the veil of ignorance that most people live in.

They are able to see, hear, feel or experience this frequency and have conversations with relatives that are dead and other entities that are still creating experiences at this level. This is a very noisy level of metaphysical experience. There are many souls operating at this level, and you can pick up a lot of static. This is the first level of the veil being removed and you are experiencing reality as it exists backstage from the physical reality. Just like in theater, you may have the actors out front on the stage, but the number of people waiting in the wings. You know, the ones that run the stage sets, costumes, dancers and lighting are all working to make the actors stay in the limelight. Their number is immense. There are hosts of traffic backstage. This is the area where shamans go to help people with healings, find guides for them and work with past lives.

The astral plane is where the extra sensory perceptions (ESP) gifts come from and you can chat with folks on the other side of the veil. It is also helpful to remember that some of the souls you will experience during this time are seeking higher planes of consciousness and they see you as someone to guide them. As I was learning to move about this level as a shaman rather than a yogi, it took me a few years to create a system to determine if a soul needed assistance to higher levels of consciousness or I was to remove them from that plane of existence. I describe this technique in my classes as, Find the Spark. There is a video about this technique in your reader bonuses.

The causal plane is not spoken of as much. It is a totally different region of experience for the mystic and it is difficult to put into words. This is the region of experience that barely has form. You still see beings moving about this level, but they are barely seen until they wish to come into your ability to see them. Then they will materialize into vague forms with a few features, so you are able to focus on a point in their form to "talk to." What I mean by this is the experiences you have here require a level of trust and vulnerability that you would never have on the physical plane.

As much as mystics desire to have this level of authenticity on the physical plane, it is nigh impossible to get this level of vulnerability on the earth plane due to all the conditions of manifestation that humans have here on the planet. The causal plane is where mystics find beings that are fully open. Literally every thought, every action, every emotion can be seen and experienced by the other. The amount of differentiation between souls is minimal and that is why the level of trust required to get to this level is so high. This is the frequency that makes communication via telepathy seem slow. I know, right? Telepathy is as slow in communication at this level as human speech is at the Astral Plane. Souls share everything at this level. Self-Identification is still present, but the intimacy at this level is complete.

I have no metaphor for this level except to say this. When we communicate with one another here in the physical realm it is equivalent to using a telegraph relative to the causal plane. Our communication on Earth is like morse code with all the challenges that presents with lots of difficulties in the transmission and reception of information and translation. The communication at the Astral plane is telepathic and emotive. You hear and feel the other souls. You hear their thoughts, and you feel their emotions at super speed and huge quantities of information are downloaded into your experience.

However, at the causal plane, your thoughts would be slow, the only emotion you experience is unconditional, expansive love. The love you experience at this level is unimaginable to someone who only remembers their physical experience. For those shamans, mediums and mystics that operate at this level they know the speed and density of information they can acquire at the astral level, but then, when you move into the causal level, that's when you move beyond the 3D version of yourself. You barely remember thought or emotion. You are standing on the border of the 4th Dimension as our current, modern physics describe it. As I sit and type this I know that it is difficult for some to understand what I am say-ing, whereas I know there are those mystics that totally know this realm. Don't worry at what point of understanding you feel you are at, because your soul knows what I am talking about and as you move through the different levels of consciousness in meditation, you'll begin to see, feel and experience what your soul wishes you to remember.

No matter what level of understanding you have of each of these levels is not the point. The purpose is that we have an understanding of the frequencies you are operating so that you are guided to your highest and best experience you can have here on planet earth while you are incarnated in a body.

Remember why you are here. You came here as a volunteer. How do I know this? Because you wouldn't be reading this book if you weren't one of those that was foretold of coming in the third wave. What is the third wave? It is a group of souls that were called from all the regions of experience. From all the levels of consciousness and creation. Earth and the humans on it had learned to build an atomic bomb and a call went out through all levels of understanding and it asked, "Who will keep them from destroying their creation?"

Volunteers were sought and you answered that call. Thank you for being here.

This book is an attempt to help you remember all that you are and to remind you of your purpose for being here.

Since you are reading this book here are some items I'd like to remind you of;

First off, **you are not here to "learn lessons" or "clear Karma**." As you read this book, please know that you are a soul who hasn't done anything wrong and you are one of the volunteers. What is the purpose of the volunteers? To live life in joy, happiness and to show others how to behave and get along with one another. We are here to ask, "Why?" Why do we hate that group? Why do we do things this way? Why are we required to do this in such a difficult way? There are easier ways to live life, aren't there?

Secondly, **you are not here to be normal**. I know that you already know that, but sometimes it helps to be reminded by a caring friend that you are not normal, so please stop thinking and choosing to be normal. You are needed as your true self. The truest self you can remember to be moment-to-moment, okay? That means you will live your life differently. Society will demand you change, family may demand you change, your children may demand that you change. Remember what your purpose in this life is. You are to live your life in freedom and joy. You are not to sacrifice your dreams for the greater good. You are not to live your life in the service of others. You are to live your life in service of bringing in as much light, love and levity as you can possibly bring moment-to-moment. That, my fellow mystic, is the greatest service you can provide. Lead others by your joy-filled life as an example.

Third, **you are supposed to be having fun.** The purpose of you being on the planet is to create the life you want, express yourself in as many creative ways as you can enjoy and to live with the freedom and abandonment as children of Divinity. I've been accused of being a member of the "happiness cult" by a few other mystics. What they didn't understand wasn't me asking you to be happy when you are miserable. What I am expressing is that you find that inner joy of Divinity that doesn't rely on what others think of you, about you or express toward you. You can find your inner spark of Divinity at any time day or night, 24/7, and your joy is not conditional on your outward surroundings. Period.

Now that we have those basics covered. Let's discuss how you move forward with all the tools, techniques, systems and processes that you know about yourself.

What type of life do you wish to create for yourself?

What sorts of fun and exciting experiences do you wish to have?

I know you've been asked that multiple times in your life, but this time this is You asking You.

We are told from multiple sources that we can do, be, have, and experience anything we want. That non-existence doesn't happen in reality and the thing we call "death" isn't a truth of our soul's journey or experience.

Much of this you already know either intuitively or logically. Most of what I have just shared you already have in your understanding. So then let's move onto the best part of you manifesting the skills that bring you the most fun.

CHAPTER 9

THE CHOICE YOU MAKE

You may have already learned this lesson, maybe not. But in case you haven't I'm going to cover this particular mindset because it is a change that occurs the more you meditate and the more in tune you are with your Divinity. Once you have this mindset firmly fixed in your day-to-day life you will find yourself free of emotional burdens and mental hiccups for a long time. The understanding is simple. You have a choice on a day-to-day basis.

You can be **right**, or you can be **happy**.

I choose to be happy.

One of the largest challenges of being an awakened soul is that you know that your life path is right for you. You're not trying to convert others to live exactly your way, because you know the folly in that reasoning. However, if you find yourself surrounded by people with large or easily threatened egos, they find your life and the way you are living as almost non-existent. You will cease to be a threat or of import in their life. The more alignment you have in your life experience, the more and more people you will see leave your sphere of influence or misbehave in a way to pull you back into the drama of their own lives. They will use your words against you, but without the profound understandings with which you uttered them.

It is then that you will realize how important it is for you to abide by your own counsel. How can anyone assist you when they have no idea the intense and profound experiences that you have personally undergone? The answer is fellow mystics can appreciate what you've been through. Other awakened souls can relate to what you've seen, heard and experienced although they will have gone through their transformation in their one way. The point is this.

You will have many people who will try to tell you how wrong you are in your belief, perspective and attitude about things, but at the core center of you-you know the one I am speaking of - the You that expresses when you are deep in meditation and the higher self-part of you that knows all about you and is the most accepting of you.

That part will share with you a novel cool way of being on the planet. This can be very threatening to anyone who has a strong paradigm of the way the world should work. Your personal perspective is not in accordance with their worldview and then you will find yourself swept up into a discussion of what is right and what is wrong.

As an enlightened soul you know the value of all perspectives and you've given up on "right" and "wrong" for the world and you only operate with those labels for yourself. What is "right" and "wrong" is more like what is appropriate for you to live your life path and what is inappropriate for you to live your life path. You've come to a higher understanding that unconditional love allows all souls to live in accordance with what they think will make them happy and not in a state of what is deemed right or wrong.

You've had many experiences already where you have had to shift your mindset. Early on in your life you received conditioning by well-meaning people who were teaching you the way the world worked. You've already had to rework those mindsets since they no longer serve you with the new experiences and understandings you are receiving from meditation. Some of your experiences have come with such deep understandings that you have memories of your soul experiences before you ever entered your body.

You know the duality that this world loves to express is a result of the choices each soul has made in the general collective.

With all that being said, it is important that you take the time each day to ask yourself, what will make me happy now?

How about now?

And now?

Because there comes a point when the enlightened soul reintegrates from the ecstatic experience of the Divine. You find yourself becoming more and more enmeshed in the fabric of three-dimensional reality and you know that it is important for you to be approachable and relatable if you are to continue on with your life path. As you move forward in your journey and as you become more and more integrated with all the remembered knowledge of All-That-You-Are, it is important that you really take control over your own life and do the things that will bring you joy, pleasure and happiness. It is easy for the enlightened souls to see the errors in the training or "domestication" as Don Miguel Ruiz states in his book, *The Four Agreements.*

Humans have undergone intense domestication as they were raised by a culture and a community that wanted them to fit in. As an awakened soul you are able to see all the layers of control, all the layers of misinformation, misunderstanding and all the areas that no longer apply to you because for you and your current understanding of reality. The rules to live by so that you can get into heaven no longer exist because you've been to heaven, you've been to hell, you've spoken to the Divine Source, you've spoken to the Darkness, you know how the fabric of reality is created, warped and woven by your thoughts, by your frequency of emotion and by your mindset.

With all this in your understanding, you know that the rules you've been living by no longer apply to you and it is important that you really know what it is you want out of life, because it is so easy for you to leave it. You've travelled beyond the astral plane. You've been to the causal plane; you've merged with Source for a bit of time and felt the touch of unconditional love in your heart and had it reverberate to the core of your being. These experiences have differentiated you in all the ways necessary that you no longer feel the drastic need to differentiate here on earth. You know your uniqueness through and through. There is no need for you to establish your differentiation here, too. It has already occurred through the very creation of you. Right?

This makes you and your life rather unremarkable to anyone who has a strong ego or needs to control their external experiences. You no longer choose to fight over what is right and what is wrong. You no longer have a need to prove yourself to others or yourself. You know to the core of your being that you are whole. You are complete. And you are worth all the love and pleasure you care to enjoy on this planet. You know without any doubt that you are worthy of love. You are worthy of joy and you set about living your life experience for the sheer joy of it. For the pleasure of it and you know that you are safely in the hands of the Divine throughout the experience.

You will be able to tell that you are bumping up against the three-dimensional version of "right" vs "wrong" when you are told to stop laughing so loud. To stop smiling so much. To stop being the happy, excited, joyful you. You will see how the people who are wanting you to stop are the ones that are still thinking that by controlling the external world around them they will be happy. You know that nothing is farther from the truth. Don't you? It is by controlling our inner world that we are able to be in a state of joy no matter what is going on in the external environment.

This is where I have had the most education of how others suffer so much. They think that if they establish enough control of their external environment they will be happy. Well, that never works, there is always more to change, more to manipulate and more to alter. Whereas, for the mystic that has control over their thoughts and their emotions, they will be the ones who seem to glide effortlessly through life. They are laughing when others are shushing them and telling them to be quiet. You can see the souls who are enjoying the sunny day, the rainy day, they are smiling while others are grumbling about the snow or the wet. You've seen these people and when you look at them, you know that internally they are at peace. They are unaffected by the external environment because something wonderful is happening within.

It could be something as simple. They could be remembering a very pleasant past experience, or they just got to make love with someone they cherish, and they are recalling the evening's entertainments. No matter what is going through the mind or emotional state of the person, the rainy day can't cloud it. Why? Because their inner world is in control of their day, not the external world.

You've had it happen to you. When you were in a really good mood, it seemed as if you were unstoppable. Nothing could go wrong. Even when you spill your coffee all over yourself and your papers, someone comes along and is there to assist you in the cleanup and a fresh copy of your paperwork was presented to you as if by magic. (Yes, I've had this happen to me.) When you're in an awful mood and things go wrong, you are left to your own devices, solutions do not present themselves as readily and you feel stuck and worried. Just remember your thoughts and your emotions are the areas you have control over, and you can pivot out of any situation that you find yourself in.

I've given you several tips for meditation, emotional control as well as thought control that have been presented by many Master Mystics. However, the strongest one that I have at my disposal, it is my breathing-diversion tactic I use with myself all the time.

This is how I use it.

Something happens that causes my thoughts or my emotions to totally spin out of control for me and I find myself becoming overwhelmed with too many thoughts or my emotions are starting a downhill race to see who can get to depression or grief faster. When any of these things start their descent for me, I notice them immediately and I do this:

- Breathe.
- I take a long inhale through my nose.
- I exhale twice out of my mouth using a huh-huh sort of sound.
- Inhale through the nose
- Exhale twice
- Inhale through the nose
- Exhale twice.

Immediately I feel better. My emotions stabilize and plateau. Now it is my mind's turn to divert my attention to the positive things in my day. I start with the basics.

I am breathing (as a childhood asthmatic, breathing was not always an assumed situation, I lived on inhalers and worried I wouldn't wake in the morning due to my awful asthma.)

I woke up this morning. (again, BONUS!)

The sun is out, and it is beautiful.

The sky is a gorgeous blue.

Birds are flying.

I hear insects calling out to one another.

Nature is my refuge, even in the concrete jungle of a major city, I can always find a patch of sky, a cloud, a flower or a tree somewhere that will divert my attention and I make sure to keep my thoughts focused on items of color and vibrancy. Nature is always with us, even if it is a picture of a place we've been, we can lose ourselves in the healing power of Mother Earth.

If I'm deep within the heart of a city, then I focus on the colors of a woman's scarf, a man's tie or a street performer's sign. There is color everywhere in our world and I can divert my mind to what is better for my world rather than what recently occurred to knock me out of alignment with my joyful self.

When I first tried working this technique in my life, I started to realize some rather uncomfortable things about myself.

The first one was, my mind enjoyed the drama. It enjoyed being a martyr and being hurt for a noble cause of being a mistreated, good person. I quickly got rid of that old stereotype left over from my catechism days in the Catholic Church.

The next thing I noticed is that sometimes my body was trying to get ill or I was mentally falling into a depression due to a misunderstanding I had about my current lifestyle. My body and emotions were telling me that this particular lesson was no longer needed as I moved forward in my current life. There were many such lessons. When I was younger, I was told that I needed meat to grow strong, that I needed dairy for healthy bones. After my awakening my diet drastically changed over the course of 3 years. To this day, I still listen to my body and emotions as I move through my day to find the right foods and balance of foods that my body needs moment to moment. One of the shocking things for those around me was how little food I consume and how little food I need to feel sated.

This is common for those who spend a great deal of time in meditation or self-introspection. The more you study yourself the more you will find that many of the routines, habits and default thinking that you have on a daily basis are, in fact, not of your own making. They were traits, behaviors and recommendations of others who do not live your life. They do not live in your body. Just remember that.

You know what is best for you. Always. You really do.

The perfect way to know what is in your personal best interest is to ask yourself how you feel about something. Even if you are a thinker like me, you can still gauge what is best for you by saying, "Well, what do I think about XYZ?" Then see how you feel. If you feel nothing. Then do not make a decision or it means that you don't have a preference one way or another. However, if someone gives you two options and one fills you with anxiety and another feels better, guess which one I'm going to ask you to go with?

The one that makes you feel better.

Please understand that the folks that try to get you to move past anxiety or fear that you may have are not living your life. Only you can truly make a choice in what is best for you because you are the one having to live with the consequences of your choices. It really is that simple.

CHAPTER 10

CHERISHED
BEYOND MEASURE

If you are reading this book, you have some form of ESP, psychic ability or spiritual gift. Guess what? It is time for you to hone your abilities.

Most of the "closet" mystics that I meet don't think that their gift should be shared for a variety of reasons. I've heard so many of the same lines over and over that I thought I would share the most common responses I've heard over the last several decades when I have encouraged others to share what they know with people.

Our job as mystics is to share what we know when asked, it is up to the person who is receiving the information from us to decide what to do with it. Also, in the communities I work with now, we also wait until someone asks us what we think or asks us for "what vibe do you get from this?" before we share.

Back in the early days of spiritualism it was common practice if Spirit said something or shared something with you the medium would be compelled to share it with the intended recipient. Even I have been compelled to break my own personal rule not to share my spiritual experiences unless asked because Spirit would shut down my ability to breathe until I said, "Okay, I'll tell them." Spirit was not being cruel. You must remember I am a very stubborn person and if I choose to follow a rule, I'll follow it until a rather significant event pops into my world to change my course. Breathing was a significant enough challenge for me that I was seriously paying attention.

Unless you have clear cut direction from Spirit on whether or not to share a spiritual understanding with someone, it is best to wait for permission or wait for a question to be asked from you directly. Giving one's consent is a big thing these days in many matters in our society, not just spiritual ones, and we as mystics have a responsibility to ourselves, to our message and to the years of developing our talents. Wait until asked. Once asked, then share what you know. The exception to this is work out a code with your HigherSelf that you need to share something when your left eye itches or something easy like that.

Because of the changes in spiritualism, mediumship and the influx of eastern philosophies, it is important that you continually practice your art or your version of mediumship or mysticism. Like any form of personal expression, it is important to stay aware of your gifts and keep them working well.

Just like an artist won't allow their canvas' to be stored incorrectly nor a musician will allow an instrument to be treated badly. You, as a mystic, need to look after your physical, emotional, mental and spiritual health. You are a cherished resource for many people who are struggling in life. You have your own challenges to be sure, but you are also on this planet to give assistance to others via the use and practice of your particular gift.

So, how do you practice your gift? By finding friends who will help you with your talent and give you questions to practice with them. Then reach out to friends of friends to see if you can practice with them. It can be scary to practice with unfamiliar people, but it is also the best way to get better at what you do. This is why so many mystics will use tarot or oracle cards for readings along with pendulums, runes, or other tools to assist them interpret the energies that are working around them.

Remember when I told you that I heard from so many mystics the various reasons why they don't want to share their gifts? Well, see if any of these excuses apply to your current resistance to practicing your art.

I Like My Life the Way It Is, I Don't Want It to Change

Many of the mystics that have shared this comment with me were on the verge of a major life change where their intuition was about to burst forth with new gifts and revelations. They would tell me to not bother them with such things and then I'd get a phone call 30-90 days later as they told me they were in need of a teacher or coach to get them through all the experiences they were going through, and they wanted someone to guide them through the trans-formative process.

One of the things I can guarantee you about your life, is that it will change. The things that I know about change is this: I have the resources, gifts and intelligence to navigate the change if I just give myself the necessary time to process the situation and allow myself the opportunity to see the situation from multiple perspectives. Then, a solution will present itself to me with an elegance and ease that I wouldn't have been able to achieve without bringing in the intuitive element. Meditate. Meditate. And if that doesn't work, Meditate!

I Don't Want to Be Seen as a Weirdo by People

You can't control how others perceive you. Period. This is something that I have had to discuss with mystics frequently for decades.

First off, you have no idea what someone thinks of you and you won't know how they will respond to you until you share your knowledge with them. It is hubris to think that you have any control over other people's thoughts, feelings or attitudes about you. That is their choice. No matter what people say or do, you may be able to affect an outcome or guide them if they allow you such a position in their life, but for the most part you have no control over what people think of you.

This is a foundational error that most of us are taught very early on. "Don't do that, you'll hurt Aunt Sally's feelings!" Or "Don't say that people will think you are uncouth." There are thousands of ways we have been taught to act or behave because of what we want other people to think about us. We believe we have control over others' opinions of us because of our training. Well, we don't.

I recommend you take some time for self-introspection and dig down in your thoughts and memories of the other things that well-meaning people may have said to you that no longer apply to you as you move forward with your spiritual journey.

It Is Time for Your Big Reveal;
It Is Time for Your Authenticity

I understand why you feel the need to protect yourself from the things you fear. I, too, spent way too many years hiding my gifts under a blanket of "logic" sounding statements.

Afterall, I was a scientist in the corporate world. Intuition is not seen with the same warmth that other occupations see it. In order for me to go with my intuition or to explain why I picked a certain process over another, I would find myself saying things like, "Oh, do you want to hear my logic on that?" As I stood before my colleagues in a departmental meeting. Most of the time my intuition gave me a nudge in the right direction, but I couldn't very well say, "Well, it felt like the right one."

By my stating, "Oh, do you wish to see my logic on that?" It gave my intuition a few seconds to come up with a line of logic that I could use to suggest that the path was a linear walk in the park. When in actuality, I experienced it as a quantum leap in my thought processes. Remember, this was the 1980s & 90s when I worked in the laboratories. With the influx of new mindsets that now exist in media, film, art and comedy, I'm sure I could get away with using more "feeling" language now than was acceptable before.

I share this with you so that you can see that there are many reasons to want to hide your gifts, but my guidance to you now is that by reading this book, it is your call. You are being asked to share more of All-That-You-Are rather than keep your bright light hidden under the proverbial wicker basket. You are needed in this world. There are many people who are just learning that they are more than just the physical, emotional and mental bodies. They need assistance with meditation, spiritual experiences and learning how to do the introspective work to release the old patterns of training that no longer suit them. They want to grow, but don't know how. We need more mystics to step up as mentors.

All that is necessary is that you get better at whatever form of spirituality you practice. If you are a medium, try doing different forms of mediumship and see which one you really enjoy and do that. If you are a card reader, try using pendulums or stones in your readings. If you are a wheel walker and you're used to changing the energies only during ceremonies, see what you can do to bring a calm, nurturing environment to a remote area.

There are many ways that you can work your gift for the benefit and betterment of humanity. We are in need of as many mystics working their craft as possible since we have a huge resurgence of new mystics coming online, seeking answers to the intense, spiritual experiences they are living. They need assistance and you have answers. Find a way to practice your craft so that others may find you.

It has never been easier to find meditation groups, online communities and helpful people through social media. It has also opened the door for naysayers, sceptics and critics. The point is, ask your intuition for guidance and you will be led to the correct group of people that will happily help you progress in your spiritual gifts and talents. There are thousands of online groups. Don't be worried that you will pick the wrong one, just go with the one that feels correct for the time and see it as a "temporary" group until you find the one that really resonates with you. You always know when you hit a point where you feel that you have fallen out of resonance with a particular group, find another one and so on and so on as you move along your spiritual journey. The point is each group will teach you a different perspective, a different set of symbols and a different mindset. As you are learning the different tools and techniques, you are constantly adding to your skill set. This is important to your development.

When you're ready for a teacher that can guide you along the path that you wish to travel, you'll know it immediately and then you can make your choices from there. But until you find the teacher you most seek at this point, wander around the spiritual and metaphysical landscape a bit looking at the various groups. There are a lot of flavors of spirituality in the world these days and there are several people that are seeking like you are.

You will be guided to the right groups for the perfect amount of time and then you will know exactly when it is time for you to move along to another group or another set of teachers. You can feel when the answers that you are being given are starting to sound route or they fall flat for you. That means there is more development that you are ready for and the current teacher you are learning from is complete.

Move along.

Now if you are in the process of doing a certification program or something like that, I recommend you stay with it to the end to get the completion, but by that time you'll know if it is important for you to get certification or not for the following few months of your life.

So many folks try too hard to "work" at their spirituality. Remember that in order to progress at your gifts and abilities it is actually a matter of relaxation and listening. Allow yourself to drift in the stream of the astral plane or the causal plane. You will need to be re-introduced to yourself by being fed spiritual knowledge, tablespoons at a time so that you are able to understand all that is being given to you.

It is a form of remembering all that you are, and you haven't been in that remembering for a very long time and like all memories they come back to you when you need them most, not when you think you need them. There is always a challenge of the timeline when it comes to spiritual aspects. Frequently, I've heard mystics discuss how the timeline is so very different for them when they meditate, receive information and then see the manifestation of their dreams later on. There are times where we feel we need the information now, but it doesn't come when we think we need it and instead it arrives when it is the most valuable to us.

There have been many times in my life when I felt incredibly alone and forsaken. I have come to understand that all souls feel abandoned at some point in their lives. When I have a student or client come to me and ask for help with abandonment issues, it causes me to laugh, not at them, but with them, because I see how we all feel abandoned at some point in our worldview. It is as if we feel so alien to the human race and we feel like we've been dumped on this planet with a bunch of barbarians and we have no idea how to get off this miserable rock. I held so much hope for the space station and for the space program as a kid. I wanted to travel the stars I wanted off and away from this place and I was working like crazy because I was so bored and tired of the day-to-day grind. Everyone around me seemed to be content and satisfied.

The point for me was that I wasn't satisfied, and I fled my hometown as soon as I was of legal age. I didn't fit in because my family wasn't from there. The point is as a military kid you never fit in, anywhere, yet you can fit in everywhere due to your training and upbringing. It is easy to adapt because you moved so much you can definitely make that happen for yourself. It is all a matter of finding out who the helpers are. Who the bullies are? Who are the crazies? I am quite fond of the crazies.

Thank you to all the souls and people who have helped me grow, expand and be complete in my process. We are always creating, building and making things happen for ourselves and we are role models for others.

You have no idea who you are going to inspire. You have no idea who is going to be helped by the work you do. That is why it is so important that you write your journey down. That you bring about the necessary knowledge that you have locked in your brain and your heart. There are people who are yet to be in your life who will benefit from all the words that you share, songs you sing and art you create.

Thank you for your psychic abilities. Thank you for continuing to practice and learn your art. You are needed in this life, my dear volunteer. Consider yourself called into service. Consider yourself Cherished-Beyond-Measure.

Please share what you know with the world. The people on the planet need your joyful creation.

CHAPTER #11

NEXT STEPS

If you've arrived at this page after reading this entire book, Thank you and congratulations! I hope I've given you enough information to inspire you to move more purposefully through your spiritual journey with a scaffolding of the gifts and perspectives available to you.

Imagine what is going to feel like to get up each day and meditate. This daily connection with your Higher Self/Source/Creator will allow you to move through your life with a grace and ease that you thought unimaginable before. If you are already a habitual meditator, I hope you've received some information on how mystics world-wide categorize and sort through the varied talents and aspects of the spiritual life.

We all know that we need meditation to stabilize and calm our experience on planet Earth, but there are times we get stubborn with ourselves and resist what is best for us. When those times occur, you have several options to move forward with a community of like-minded friends or you can be inspired by the videos and podcasts of people who are here to uplift the frequency of humankind with positive messages of courageous mystics.

Ready to Get Started?

When you are ready to get started with any of my programs the first step is to go to our community's website and schedule a 15-minute zoom meeting with me so that we can acknowledge the many spiritual traits you possess and assist you with building upon the foundation you've already created for yourself. Remember every important and valuable journey begins with this critical first step.

Schedule a session with me today and get started on the process of creating what I think is one of the smartest and most valuable investments you can make in yourself, which is committing time to aligning with your higher purpose through meditation and community support.

My coaching programs and meditation systems are an investment and definitely not for everybody. But relative to the multitude of other ways you can invest in your spiritual understanding, my Mystic MasterMind and 3 Minute Meditation Programs are a bargain and give you hugely (big brain word there) valuable life skills and techniques that you can leverage for the rest of your life here on planet Earth.

I am a firm believer that you are uniquely qualified to be working with certain people. Not everybody will "get" you or what you do or what you stand for. I know that is totally true for me. In order for us to see if we are a good fit, I have a simple and easy way to further explore this opportunity and it all starts with a 15-min Zoom session between you and me. This will give us a chance to "meet" and see if working together makes sense. To schedule a call here is what to do:

1. Visit https://thepracticalmystics.com/
2. Review my videos, articles and programs.
3. Click "Connect" and follow the prompts to schedule a chat.

This one-to-one call will help me understand what you do and what your goals are. This call is all about helping you decide if working together to get your meditation schedule and spiritual systems in place is a good fit for both of us. It's a two-way interview to make sure we agree this is a good match.

I look forward to hearing from you, and more importantly, working together to turn you into a

Spiritual Dynamo who is in total alignment with your purpose and knows what is best for yourself with every decision you make for your life path.

ABOUT JANINE BOLON

J anine is a testament to the power of perseverance. As an impoverished teenager in rural Missouri, she launched several successful businesses before putting herself through the University of Missouri biochemistry program by working three jobs at once and selling all her possessions.

She worked for 15 years in academic and industrial research laboratories before spending the next 20 years raising a brood of four active spawn. In the past two decades, Janine has completed her M.A. in Education, home-schools the herd, started another entrepreneurial venture (The8Gates, LLC., a firm dedicated to teaching fundamental principles of spiritual and financial independence), has written nine books on the topic and teaches math and metaphysics in her spare time. Janine's new book coming out in February 2022, *Creating with the Divine: Building a Business for the Spiritually Gifted*, describes the systems and day-to-day behaviors needed to practice your spiritual gifts full time while making money to live well. Janine has been working from home for over 25+ years and describes how to live, work and enjoy a self-created life steeped in meditation, joy and adventure.

THE PRACTICAL MYSTIC SHOW

The Practical Mystic Show is an interview style podcast where Janine and other mystics from all over the world discuss their spiritual gifts, the challenges they have faced and how they have managed to create the life of their own choosing through the use of their dreams, vision, meditations and business acumen.

This show was started in 2017 at the behest of a friend who wanted to hear more "stories" about mystics. In 2020 The Practical Mystic Show became syndicated and is now available on 27 different platforms including iTunes, Spotify, Podbean & Pandora services.

Check it out on https://thepracticalmystics.com/ podcast and if you think you'd make a suitable guest, visit:

https://thepracticalmystics.com/guest

Connect with our production crew so we can get you on our broadcast schedule!

ANNOTATED BIBLIOGRAPHY

Here are some books that have helped me greatly in my spiritual journey. These resources will not be able to replace meditation for developing personal experiences with Source, but they offer reassurance that you are not alone on your path. Many types of mystics have been successful at self-discovery even in the face of major challenges. These are the inspirational books that helped me stay on track:

Ask and It is Given, Esther and Jerry Hicks. If you enjoy a book that teaches and then gives you honest-to-goodness practice steps, this is for you. When I read this book in 2015, I loved how the exercises walked you through different types of systems for thinking through your self-limiting beliefs and emotions. There are over twenty-two different systems to choose from for making your life better.

Autobiography of a Yogi, Paramahansa Yogananda. This landmark book that got me into a spiritual form of discipline that would last the rest of my life. Not everyone is as single-minded as I am when it comes to goal setting, but Yogananda's experiences with his awakening are eloquently described, giving you another example of what it means to engage in life and still keep a quietness of mind amidst chaos.

How We Die: Reflections on Life's Final Chapter, Sherwin B. Nuland. I read this book in 1995 when I was doing a lot of coaching on going through grief. It was a great reminder that we will all die and it is up to us to figure out what that needs to look like. After considering the way my mom died, I was better able to make choices on how I wanted to die after reading this book. The latest edition has an added chapter on the current practices in health care and ways that you might want your family to work with you should you develop a terminal illness or one of the seven major diseases that can be terminal. Yes, the book was written twenty years ago, but not much has changed in the process of dying, only the amount of control patients now have in their care.

The Law of Attraction: The Basics of the Teachings of Abraham, Esther and Jerry Hicks. I didn't read this book until 2014 when a friend gave it to me and told me much of what I was teaching was also in this book. Well, let's just say I devoured this book as the authors explain, in clear, concise secular language, a spiritual path devoid of religious entanglements and the practice of the path involved. A wonderful book!

Life in the World Unseen, Anthony Borgia. This book is a pleasant perspective of the afterlife as experienced by Monsignor Robert Hugh Benson. He shared his perspective with Borgia after he died. Benson's belief that he and the other souls he sees will continue their spiritual evolution for all eternity in the afterlife realm is in contradiction to my own life experiences with reincarnation, but that does not negate this book or the poetic mind of Monsignor Benson. For people who are just learning about the afterlife, I recommend this as a solid starting point.

The Power of Myth, Joseph Campbell. Campbell experienced enlightenment at the age of 27 and spent the rest of his life using academic scholarship and lectures to teach what he knew. He was brilliant at integrating the stories and legends of tribal peoples all over the world and using their metaphors to create purposeful stories for his readers, students and community. This book helped me incorporate the

Greek, Roman, and Hindu perspectives into my Christian metaphors as I moved along my spiritual path. Campbell also helped me overcome the frustrations of fitting language to transcendent experiences.

The 4 Agreements, Don Miguel Ruiz. This book is what I recommend to all mystics that wish to build a community of any kind. Whether it is online, in person or you have retreats. When you get ready to move out into the world and organize people for a group enterprise, The 4 Agreements, is a great foundation to keep participants in understanding of what we expect from them and what they can expect from us as facilitators.

The Power of Now, Ekhart Tolle. For those that struggle with wayward thoughts and challenging mental trash talk that goes on in your head. You will love how Tolle works with people and shares with them how to get out of their own way and to give up the concept that "You are your Mind." He proves to you step-by-step that you are not your thoughts. I've read this book more as an audiobook. I would go to sleep listening to Ekhart talk about his methods and personal journey. No matter what format you choose to use with this book, you'll not be remiss in absorbing the information within.

GLOSSARY OF TERMS
JANINE USES

B elow are all the words I've had my students, beta readers and editors ask me to describe in better detail. This is a common problem with modern English. There are so many terms we have borrowed from other languages or customs that the way I use a word may not be the same as you use it. Here are the meanings I have for the following words:

Catechism, a summary of the principles of Christian religion in the form of questions and answers, used for the instruction of Christians. Before I was given confirmation and my first communion, I had to attend months of classes with the nuns learning the prayers, questions and answers of the Roman Catholic Church.

Compassion, concern for the sufferings and misfortunes of others. I encourage most people to operate with a sense of compassion toward others rather than empathy. I teach health care professionals the difference between sympathy, empathy and compassion so that they can remain in a state of compassion without becoming burdened in the lower emotional states of sympathy and empathy. As spiritual beings experiencing the range of emotions of human life, it behooves us to stay connected to others through our compassion, but not allow our own emotions to be triggered or involved in a person's suffering. We cannot offer the greatest help to them if we don't vibrate at a higher rate while they are in a vibration of pain. By offering our higher frequency to merge with their frequency, we remind the soul of where they will feel better. It is important as a healer of any kind, to remind the souls that come to us for help that their origin is of a higher vibration, and that our duty as their consultant, mystic or healer, is to remind them of their own power to heal themselves. We offer suggestions on systems, resources, and techniques, but the healing is their own responsibility of listening to their higher guidance for the soul knows how to heal the body.

Diksha, the laying on of hands by a guru in blessing, the transfer of spiritual gifts or spiritual dispensation. This is a ceremonial blessing that has been used for centuries in many different countries. I first experienced it in a Hindu Temple in Colorado by Sai Maa before my diksha by Christ.

Empathy, the ability to feel what another person is feeling, Most of my life I was taught that empathy was the ability to understand what another was feeling. I have since changed my personal definition. There are people on this planet that totally have the ability to literally feel other people's emotions. They often get confused on "what is mine and what is theirs" as they grow up around others. This confusion is what causes some empaths to become introverts or people-pleasers in an effort to feel better. Empaths will often do whatever they can to help others feel better. Most of our medical professionals are empaths. There are techniques that a person can use to define when an emotion is their own or someone else's.

Grandfather of the West, a spiritual guide in many Native American traditions who is the keeper of time, the guardian of ancient wisdom and gate-keeper of spiritual gifts. He is the primary teacher to Sacred Clowns and assists shamans with healings in ceremonies. Grandfather of the West is a metaphor I have seen in many religions as the entity of Death, but it doesn't necessarily mean a physical death. I came to learn that he also represented Bat Medicine (think Plato's cave) of certain shamans who would undergo a spiritual death ceremony as they came into their psychic gifts as healers and mediums.

Sympathy, feelings of pity or sorrow for someone else's misfortune. This situation or emotion is a conditioned response we have for others. It is the first step in offering understanding to those around us. We are taught from a young age that if someone tells us something awful has happened to them, loss of job, death in the family, divorce or natural disaster, we are to offer them condolences if we have no other means of assistance.

PERSONAL NOTES

(I write in books when I read them, I wanted you to have
some pages to record your thoughts too!)

WELCOME & THANK YOU!

Your investment in this book entitles you to a special gift that is the perfect companion to *Expressing the Divine.*

It is a group of videos that assist with meditation, expansion of your personal skills as well as a checklist to see what skills you may already possess and which ones you may be ready to improve.

This collection of media will allow you to study and improve your own metaphysical gifts in greater detail!

DOWNLOAD TODAY!

ThePracticalMystics.com/thanks

Made in the USA
Monee, IL
21 September 2022

14313461R00089